'72

TIME PRESENT

THE HOTEL IN AMSTERDAM

Other Plays by John Osborne

*

A BOND HONOURED

LUTHER

INADMISSIBLE EVIDENCE

A PATRIOT FOR ME

LOOK BACK IN ANGER

THE ENTERTAINER

PLAYS FOR ENGLAND :
The Blood of the Bambergs and *Under Plain Cover*

A SUBJECT OF SCANDAL AND CONCERN :
A play for television

EPITAPH FOR GEORGE DILLON
(with Anthony Creighton)

TOM JONES : A FILMSCRIPT

Time Present
The Hotel in Amsterdam

by

JOHN OSBORNE

FABER AND FABER
24 Russell Square
London

First published in 1968
by Faber and Faber Limited
24 Russell Square London WC1
Reprinted 1968
Printed in Great Britain by
Latimer Trend & Co Ltd Plymouth
All rights reserved

SBN 571 08537 7 (Paper covers)
SBN 571 08536 9 (Cloth)

"A time to embrace and a time to refrain from embracing. A time to get and a time to lose: a time to keep, and a time to cast away."

ECCLESIASTES

CAST

EDITH
PAULINE
CONSTANCE
PAMELA
MURRAY
EDWARD
BERNARD
ABIGAIL

TIME PRESENT
A Play

ACT ONE

CONSTANCE'S *flat in Pimlico. For the present she is sharing it with* PAMELA. *There is some evidence that it is lived in by two people with different temperaments and interests. On the whole, the impression is rather severe, more a working area than a place to lounge around. The influence of* CONSTANCE *is in the Scandinavian furniture and abstracts. There is also the evidence of her profession of M.P. There is a wall of books, reports, white papers, volumes of Hansard, Year Books, filing cabinets and hundreds of back numbers of political weeklies, all very neatly arranged for reference. There is a prominent, large Swedish desk covered with still more books, newspapers, reports, galley proofs and a typewriter with paper in it. A glass table with a large selection of drinks, a record player, a television set. Records on the floor (*PAMELA'S *untidiness). A couple of modish, uncomfortable steel and leather chairs. Two doors leading to bedrooms. A partitioned kitchen full of jars for exotic herbs, chopping boards, wine racks, business-like knives, strings of garlic and so on. In the less severe part of the room there are Japanese lampshades, a day-bed and a pile of expensive looking clothes wrapped in plastic covers, clearly just back from the cleaners. On one wall on this side is an old poster. It says simply* "NEW THEATRE, HULL. GIDEON ORME—MACBETH—WITH FULL LONDON CAST etc". *On the table is a rather faded production photograph of an ageing but powerful-looking actor in Shakespearian costume. It is late at night and when the curtain rises* EDITH, PAMELA'S *mother, is sitting on one of the uncomfortable chairs with a cup of tea and reading a copy of Hansard. She is in her late fifties, and looks tired but alert. The doorbell rings. She goes to it and calls out firmly before opening.*

EDITH: Who is it?
VOICE: Mummy? It's Pauline.
    (*She admits* PAULINE, *her youngest daughter, who is about eighteen and pretty.*)

EDITH: I thought Pamela gave you a spare key.

PAULINE: She wouldn't.

EDITH: Wouldn't?

PAULINE: No.

EDITH: Well, why not? She gives them round to all sorts of peculiar people.

PAULINE: Don't know. Thinks I'm going to have a rave up while she and Connie are out I expect. Any news?

EDITH: I rang about twenty minutes ago. Pamela's been with him since eight o'clock. She said he was a bit quieter. Whatever that means. He always seems to chatter whenever she's there. She lets him go on and on then gets more exhausted than ever. By the time I get there, he complains all the time about how tired he is and can't sleep. Why am I so tired, Edith? I haven't done any work for years. Not since I was at the Shaftesbury. He even got that wrong last night. That was long before the war. He complained all the time just before *I* left. Are you sure you want to come? It's not much fun, darling. You know, sitting up all night in a hospital room.

PAULINE: No, I'll come.

EDITH: Want some tea before we go?

PAULINE: No, thanks.

EDITH: I've got a flask for us. That night sister, not the other one, she's not very concerned for your comfort.

PAULINE: Glad I'm not a patient. I've never been ill in bed. It must be a bit odd.

EDITH: Yes, you have. You've had measles and tonsilitis. And very badly.

PAULINE: Yes, but I don't remember that. I mean being ill, like a, like an experience, lying there. Wondering what they're going to do to you if you're going to get up. So he complains?

EDITH: Nurses, the doctors, the food, the bed, oh everything.

PAULINE: He never says anything to me much. Oh, he looked at me a long time Tuesday night and then just asked me if I took drugs.

EDITH: Oh, he asks me silly questions.

14

PAULINE: He said would I get some for him. What'd he ask you?

EDITH: Oh, nothing. I think he often doesn't know what year it is. He thinks he's still on the stage or that we're still married. You really needn't come you know.

PAULINE: I know.

EDITH: Pamela's *his* daughter. He's made that *very* clear. And besides it's different with him and her.

PAULINE: Hello, reading the old Hansard?

EDITH: Yes.

PAULINE: Daddy?

EDITH: No, Constance.

PAULINE: Ah. Any good?

EDITH: I should think so. Not exactly my subject. "New Humber and Fisheries Development Act". Second reading.

PAULINE: I should think not.

EDITH: One of the brightest of the last batch. So Daddy says. Perhaps we should ask her to dinner one evening. When all this is over.

PAULINE: Odd fish for Pamela to shack up with.

EDITH: How do you mean?

PAULINE: Oh, I don't know but I suppose she's frightfully intellectual and an M.P. and all that. And—well, I mean, Pamela's an actress.

EDITH: She's not exactly unintelligent, darling. Even if she does get her life in a bit of a mess. And I think Constance has been kind to her and after that last affair bust up and all.

PAULINE: What? Oh, Alec. But that was for years. Like marriage. Worse.

EDITH: And I think she genuinely admires Pamela. As an actress. And *she* says Constance is the only person who's really encouraged her in her work. Which is true. I used to take an interest. But I had two younger children. And your father's impossible to get to a theatre.

PAULINE: Didn't the old man encourage her?

EDITH: Well, with her own father it was complicated of course. I could never make out what he really wanted for Pamela, being such a famous actor. But then when I said she ought

15

to get a good degree and a profession, he wasn't too keen on that either. Still, she might have spent fifteen years or so, like I did, training her mind to end up washing nappies and getting up coal.

PAULINE: Did you mind much?

EDITH: Of course I minded. Well, I had three children. But of course, I minded. One always minds waste. And the worst waste I can think of is training a woman to the top of her potential and then just off-loading her into marriage when she's probably at her most useful. Probably at the height of her powers.

PAULINE: Well, you can't say Pam's done that.

EDITH: No, but then she's an actress. I meant someone like, well, like Constance is a good example.

PAULINE: Do you think she'll end up first woman Prime Minister?

EDITH: She's got a very good chance of being a Cabinet Minister. Well, so Daddy says, and she's always in the papers. Still, Pamela hasn't done too badly. Having a famous father may not have always helped her. It's hard to tell. They either expect too much of you or compare you unfavourably. She should have done better.

PAULINE: Perhaps they don't write the parts. I mean Pamela's a bit special too, isn't she?

EDITH: How do you mean?

PAULINE: Well, she's not a raving beauty exactly but she's not ugly but you don't quite know what to *do* with her. I suppose it doesn't matter these days. But she's been at it a long time. I mean years.

EDITH: I wonder if she'll want some tea.

PAULINE: I mean I remember coming up to London to see her play Titania *years* ago. I was a little kid. I'd just started school.

EDITH: I don't remember.

PAULINE: She wasn't very good.

EDITH: If you were so young, you wouldn't have known. I thought she was excellent. And a beautiful costume.

PAULINE: You just said you didn't remember.

16

EDITH: Well, I do now. I'm tired. It's these long waiting
     sessions with Gideon. And that place is so freezing.
PAULINE: Would you like me to go for you tonight? I don't
     mind.
EDITH: That's very sweet of you, darling. But I think it has to
     be me. Me or Pamela. I think it's all right for you and
     Andrew to help out in the daytime.
PAULINE: I don't think he likes me all that much.
EDITH: I don't know if he really wants anyone with him. He's
     certainly not particularly pleased to see me. He usually just
     grunts when I go in or makes me do something for him.
     Make him comfortable or change his pillows. Or sometimes
     he just looks away as if he's not seen me . . Pamela, I
     suppose. He must want her with him. But he's harsh with
     her too sometimes, I've heard him.
PAULINE: He's jolly old.
EDITH: He's only seventy-two for heaven's sake, Pauline.
PAULINE: Well, if you don't think that's old—
EDITH: Well, I'm fifty-eight. I suppose you think I'm half in the
     grave.
PAULINE: No. But the old boy really seems different somehow.
     Different scene altogether. What else did he ask about?
EDITH: Gideon? Oh, oh, he rambled. I think he thought I was
     some actor-manager he used to know. Kept talking about
     seeing the returns, and the week—and then he asked, well,
     if Daddy, and I still made love to each other.
PAULINE: What did you say?
EDITH: Asked me in front of the nurse. Anyway, he didn't
     really want to know.
PAULINE: No?
EDITH: He was never a jealous man. Sexually, I mean. They
     said that's why he was no good as Othello. He simply
     couldn't understand. I'd say he was pretty free of all
     jealousy. But then he's rather a simple man in many ways.
PAULINE: And do you?
EDITH: What?
PAULINE: What he asked you. You know, Daddy?
EDITH: Good heavens, Pauline, I've told you, I'm not a zombie

B   17

just because I'm not *your* age any longer.

PAULINE: Sorry.

(CONSTANCE *lets herself in. She is in her early thirties. Bulging briefcase.*)

EDITH: Hello, Constance. I'm sorry we're still here.

CONSTANCE: Please. You're welcome. Did you get yourself anything? Hello, Pauline.

PAULINE: Hi.

EDITH: All I wanted, thanks. I usually have something in the waiting room—just a sandwich or something—and either Andrew or Pauline go in with him for a few minutes. Just to give me a break. But it's very good of them. Hospital rooms aren't places for young people to hang about.

CONSTANCE: There are worse places.

EDITH: But it's such a help being able to come over here and put my feet up while Pamela's taking over. Otherwise it takes me an age to get home.

CONSTANCE: How is he?

EDITH: All right. I spoke to Pamela about half an hour ago. She should be back now.

CONSTANCE: Who'll be there in the meantime?

EDITH: Andrew. It'll only be for ten minutes.

CONSTANCE: Isn't there a night nurse?

EDITH: Yes, but she's not there all the time. I mean they can't be of course. And he panics if he's left alone. Especially if he nods off and there's no one there when he wakes up.

CONSTANCE: It must be frightening, especially at this time of night.

EDITH: He won't trust anyone, I'm afraid. He's convinced he's going to be alone.

CONSTANCE: Not even Pamela?

EDITH: Yes. I suppose he *does* trust her?

CONSTANCE: And no improvement?

EDITH: There's always hope I suppose.

CONSTANCE: I wish that were true.

EDITH: One has to carry on on that basis. You look tired yourself.

CONSTANCE: Looked like being an all night sitting for an awful

18

moment.

PAULINE: Did you speak to Daddy?

CONSTANCE: We had a coffee together. He said he'd pick up Andrew from the hospital.

EDITH: We'd better go. He'll be tired too. Where's Pamela got to!

CONSTANCE: Perhaps I'd better get her some scrambled eggs or something. How did she sound?

EDITH: Um?

CONSTANCE: On the phone.

EDITH: Oh, all right. Not very communicative. Old men can be very wearing indeed. Especially in these circumstances. I know what he's like with me. But with Pamela it's even worse. (*Pause.*) I don't think he's really afraid.

CONSTANCE: No?

EDITH: No.

CONSTANCE: Isn't everyone?

EDITH: No, I don't think so.

CONSTANCE: Especially when you're in full possession of all your faculties. It isn't as if he's drugged stupid.

PAULINE: He wishes he was.

CONSTANCE: Pamela tells me he talks endlessly. And makes jokes.

EDITH: He doesn't know who I am half the time. I know it. He's *very* difficult to understand.

CONSTANCE: Really? He sounded rather coherent from what Pamela said to me.

EDITH: Well, I don't know about that. I only know what I see.

CONSTANCE: He is, he is dying isn't he?

EDITH: I suppose so.

CONSTANCE: Does anyone know?

EDITH: You know what they're like. They're not interested. Especially if you're what they call "the relatives". They make it pretty clear what a nuisance you are—just the fact that you exist.

CONSTANCE: Can *I* do anything at all?

EDITH: I don't think so, thank you, Constance. My husband's as well placed as—

19

CONSTANCE: I know. Of course. But, well, you know what I feel for Pamela, and I hate to feel there's so little I can do to help her.

EDITH: You're her friend. That's enough. She needs friends. Without her father. Well, she'll find it harder still. (*Pause.*) *We're* not friends. She and I, I mean. Well, certainly not like Pauline and Andrew and I are friends. In an odd way, we three seem to be more like the same generation. We understand each other. Perhaps it's just the old problem of remarrying and having more children. Something happens. It's different with the other child. It must be. However intelligent you try to be. I think that's true isn't it, Pauline? Or am I deceiving myself? Pamela seems in the middle somewhere.

PAULINE: No. That's right I guess.

CONSTANCE: Can I ask you?

EDITH: Well?

CONSTANCE: About Sir Gideon. What are your feelings about him?

EDITH: Gideon hasn't been my husband for over twenty years.

CONSTANCE: It seems strange when you put it like that.

EDITH: It's the fact. We went separate ways long ago. Not that our ways were ever joined particularly. He was a lot older than me, you see.

CONSTANCE: Yes.

EDITH: And he was also famous long before I met him, I never even saw him play very much I suppose. . . . I had a degree in English and French and . . . oh, well, all long past history. Where do you suppose she's got to? We'll go, I think.

CONSTANCE: She probably walked.

(*Enter* PAMELA. *She is in her early thirties too.*)

PAMELA: Hello. Hello, Edith. I walked.

EDITH: Are you all right, darling?

PAMELA: Oh, all right.

CONSTANCE: Sure? Something to eat? I'm getting some. Scrambled eggs?

(*She shakes her head.*)

20

Tea?

PAMELA: No, thanks. I'll have a glass of champagne.

CONSTANCE (*to others*): Are you sure you won't have something. You've got a long night.

EDITH: We must be going.

(*But she doesn't move. The attention of all of them is on* PAMELA, *as if she had brought danger or ill fortune with her. She waits. Sees her clothes.*)

PAMELA: Ah, the old plunder's back from the cleaners. At last. What's left of it.

EDITH: How is he?

PAMELA: Chatty.

EDITH: Still?

PAMELA: Don't worry. Andrew's boring him to death quite literally. About being turned on and dropping out and all.

EDITH: I don't know what I'd have done without Andrew in that place.

PAMELA: Constance, would you open it? I'm too exhausted. That bog faced night nurse hadn't put any in the fridge. You have some, Mother. It'll get you through.

EDITH: No. Thank you. We must go.

(*Pause.*)

PAMELA: Rested?

EDITH: Not much.

PAMELA: You should take a pill. I do. Don't look so glum. I tell you, he'll have quietened down by the time you get there.

EDITH: He'll wake. He always does. How is he *really*?

PAMELA: How do I know? Sometimes I think he'll live forever. He'll last tonight. Why pretend?

(CONSTANCE *pours champagne.*)

PAMELA: That's what I want. That's what he wanted, poor darling. Constance?

CONSTANCE: No, I'm making tea.

PAMELA: Oh, go on. For my sake if not yours.

CONSTANCE: All right then, I will.

PAMELA: Mother?

(EDITH *hesitates.*)

21

Andrew's all right. He's having a bedside happening all to himself. Papa's pretending to be asleep. He might even drop off with the effort. I won't offer you any, Pauline. She doesn't approve of alcohol, do you? Haven't got any L.S.D. to offer you.

PAULINE: Thanks, Pamela. I think I will have a glass.

PAMELA: Oh, good. Unless Constance has got some pot upstairs. Didn't your lover leave his tin behind the last time? There! Nothing vulgar. Just good trusty old Moet. Her lover drinks nothing but Dom Perignon. Very vulgar. Oh, that's better. (*To* CONSTANCE.) Did you vote or divide or whatever? (*She nods.*) Don't tell me—you won. What were the figures.

CONSTANCE: 245–129.

PAMELA: Surprise. Like playing for matches really isn't it? (*To* PAULINE.) I suppose that hippie outside belongs to you?

EDITH: Who?

PAMELA: Does he have a name or is he a group? It was a bit difficult to tell if he was one or several.

PAULINE: You know perfectly well.

EDITH: Did you bring Dave, darling?

PAULINE: He doesn't mind waiting.

EDITH: You should have brought him up.

PAMELA: No, she was quite right.

PAULINE: He's O.K., Mummy. He said he'd come with us.

EDITH: You know Pamela.

PAMELA: Well enough. Anyway, Constance has just had her nice carpet cleaned.

PAULINE: So what are you supposed to be proving?

PAMELA: I'm just enjoying my first drink of the evening.

PAULINE: Just bitchy and you know it.

PAMELA: You see, you really don't know me. But no loss. For either of us.

EDITH: Are you sure you haven't had a drink?

PAMELA: I told you.

EDITH: You do seem—a bit exhilarated.

PAMELA: I walked through the side streets. No Andrew.

EDITH: I shouldn't stay up, Pamela.

PAMELA: *You've* never been an actor. One needs to wind down.

PAULINE: Have you been performing then?

PAMELA: No, but my papa has. You don't think someone will tow Dave away if you leave him?

PAULINE: Oh, you're a drag—

PAMELA: Looks pretty high to me.

EDITH: What's the matter with him?

PAMELA: He's on what your children call a trip, Mama. Having unmemorable visions in a psychedelic, sort of holiday camp shirt and a racoon coat in my doorway. Trip clothes, right, Pauline?

PAULINE: You just hate any sort of fun or anything.

PAMELA: Give him the trip home, will you, darling? And I don't think it's such fun taking Dave, Dave for an all night rave in hospital, so just get your skates on will you and get rid of him?

PAULINE: No. I'm not going to.

PAMELA: Don't look at your Mother. Do as *I* tell you. I'm bigger than you.

PAULINE: And he's bigger than you. So *you* get rid of him.

CONSTANCE: Shall I go down?

EDITH: It's not necessary. We're going.

PAMELA: Not with him you're not. My Father was always very particular about who visited him. Whether it was at home or at work. Getting into his dressing room was like going into Fort Knox. And I don't see why he should be invaded by Dave the Rave. Hippie Andrew's bad enough.

CONSTANCE: I'll speak to him.

PAMELA: No, you won't. He'll be back in the doorway tomorrow night if you chat him up. Pauline—

PAULINE: You kill me. You're a provincial.

PAMELA: Very likely. As your Mother will remember, I was born in India. It's where a lot of us come from. Just as you like then. I'll call the law.

PAULINE: Oh, come off it. (*To* EDITH.) I'll have a word with him.

EDITH: Well, do hurry then. Pamela may be right. Perhaps just the two of us.

PAMELA: Just send him back where you found him. Where was it? The Sidcup Rave Cave. Yes?

PAULINE: Get lost, draggy.

PAMELA: I'll get the law, if you don't move, darling.

EDITH: Oh, stop sniping at the girl, Pamela.

PAULINE: We just do fun things, so what's the matter with *you*, then?

EDITH: But do tell him, darling. Or else let me go on my own. Perhaps that's the best idea.

PAULINE: No, you can't stay up on your own.

PAMELA: Well?

EDITH: I don't think I even remember Dave.

PAMELA: Why should you? He's an American. You met him, Constance. He's been here before. He writes a regular column—when he's not too high—for the farthest out paper. The "Village What". Sorry, that's just what it's called. Don't you remember: thought London was on the way to being the leadingest place, round the clock city, oh and for freak-outs, cats, chicks, soul groups, and pushing things, like the senses as far as they will go.

CONSTANCE: Oh, that one.

PAMELA: Has a very bad skin.

PAULINE: So what about it? What's so wrong about a bad skin? Why should we change what we really are for you? What are *you*, anyway?

PAMELA: Just a gipsy, dear, that's all. And I don't think blackheads or spots are exactly an aesthetic, whatsit imperative.

PAULINE: All that's finished.

PAMELA: I forgot. He also plays the finger-cymbals. Seven thousand people came to hear him accompany his fellow poets at the Albert Hall.

PAULINE: You wouldn't know a clarinet if you saw one.

PAMELA: Where did seven thousand beautiful people come from, he said. Did he say that to you?

CONSTANCE: Repeatedly.

PAMELA: They were all hideously self-conscious and ugly, I'm afraid. Just like Dave.

PAULINE: You don't know it yet, Pamela, but you'll wake up to it, all your scene is really out, and it'll be out for good and you with it.

PAMELA: I think you're right.

PAULINE: Those draggy plays. Who wants them?

PAMELA: Who's arguing?

PAULINE: Oh—you're just camp.

PAMELA: So I've been told. Just like my father. I wish I could say the same for you. It's impossible to argue with someone wearing such cheap clothes. Take a glass of champagne down to Dave. He doesn't *need* to look quite so ugly, you know. I suppose he thinks *he's* beautiful, of course.

CONSTANCE: Do you want me to come with you?

PAMELA: Why not? You're a party authority on education or about to be or something. You could, let's see, you could try to apply the problems of relating poetry, freak-outs, crazy slides, happenings, action painting and so on to the Comprehensive School. Or the Grammar School. Or trip clothes. She actually sells those things she's wearing. What's the name of the shop? Switched Off or Knocked Off or something. Oh, no, I forgot, that's finished now isn't it? The shoddy clothes scene. It's the bookshop, she sells books and records and dope I shouldn't wonder. "Ecstatic" that's the name of that one. "Ecstatic". And there's an art gallery attached. Quite a scene, isn't it, Pauline. And then there's her pad in the evenings.

EDITH: She's helping me through a very difficult time, darling.

PAMELA: Is she? What time is that?

EDITH: What's the matter with you?

PAMELA: What difficult time?

EDITH: Gideon's illness, you stupid girl, what else?

PAMELA: You're doing all right. It's nearly over. Her pad, where she raves in the evening, whatever you might wonder that is, getting laid, I suppose, well, now and then, lying about mostly, getting high in her pad, which is just a bed-sitter full of unappealing modish junk and old laundry.

EDITH: I'll ring you at the usual time. Try and get some sleep.

25

You've been too long in that little room.

CONSTANCE: Perhaps I could go. Tomorrow?

PAMELA: She could take over from you.

EDITH: That's not necessary. Poor Andrew—he'll be wondering. Goodnight, Constance. Do go to bed Pamela.

PAMELA: I'm not tired. Goodnight, Mama. I'll see you in the morning . . . you'll ring me?

EDITH: Yes, I've told you.

PAMELA: No, I don't mean leave it to Pauline or Andrew. You'll get straight through yourself. You will?
(EDITH *nods*.)
Anyway, I don't think anything'll happen tonight. Goodnight, Pauline.

PAULINE: Goodnight.

PAMELA: Wave to Dave for me.

EDITH: Why don't you take your own advice and have a pill?

PAMELA: I probably shall. Goodnight, Mama.
((*Pause. They go out.* CONSTANCE *closes the door on them.*)
Thank God! They've gone! We must be *going*. Why didn't she *go*? Instead of drinking champagne and going on about it, being so busy looking tired and distressed. She's Madam Distress Fund, my Mama. Calling her Mama is better than Edith. Edith almost makes her sound dignified.

CONSTANCE: I suppose she hasn't had much sleep for quite a while. None of you have.

PAMELA: They don't need it. My Mother's a bat, and, as for the kids, they're only half conscious most of the day or night so, as they'd say, who needs sleep. *I* need sleep. Lots of it. I sleep my life away. Or I would if I could. Now *we* can talk. Have some more. How are *you*?

CONSTANCE: I'm all right. I've been worried about you.

PAMELA: At least she didn't call you Connie. I've got her out of that. Do they call you Connie in the Party? I'll bet they do.

CONSTANCE: Some of them.

PAMELA: Does lover?

CONSTANCE: No. I thought it was test number one.

PAMELA: Yes. I should say, I should say it probably was. They don't bring out the best in me. If there's a best nailed down under somewhere. Not even you, not much.

CONSTANCE: Your worst can be pretty attractive.

PAMELA: I can't think that's true. I think you believe it though.

CONSTANCE: I don't want to sound like your Mother, sorry—
Mama, Edith or whatever you like, but I think you *should*
get some sleep.

PAMELA: Yes. In a minute.

CONSTANCE: I suppose they've dealt with Dave?

PAMELA: Oh, he's harmless.

CONSTANCE: How was it?

PAMELA: How was what?

CONSTANCE: Your Father?

PAMELA: Oh, all right.

CONSTANCE: Was he chatty?

PAMELA: Not very.

CONSTANCE: Darling, you're exhausted. Why don't you let me
go first thing? Just at the beginning. You could have an
extra couple of hours. Your Mother wouldn't mind.

PAMELA: Why should she? *He* might.

CONSTANCE: I see.

PAMELA: I told you. He's particular.

CONSTANCE: No. Well, I suppose I don't really know him.

PAMELA: He'll grumble at her a bit. If he's able.

CONSTANCE: You look afraid.

PAMELA: Do I? I'm not panicky, if that's what you mean.

CONSTANCE: No, I didn't. . . .

PAMELA: I held his hand mostly. I brought him some caviare but
he didn't want it . . . I just couldn't stay any longer. I
knew I couldn't get rid of her once her turn came. He
won't like it if it's tonight. She can make the
"arrangements" anyway. What do you do? Ring that place
in Ken. High Street. Well, she'll enjoy all that. Great
organiser, Mama. Great, sloppy minded organiser. She'll be
telling young Pauline that I'm over tired and strained. What
she means is venomous and evil tongued and selfish.

CONSTANCE: Well, you're not. So do shut up.

PAMELA: Oh I *am* selfish. I won't give money to take full page
ads about Vietnam or organise them like Mama. I certainly

27

wouldn't give money. I'm too mean. Too mean and too poor. Just because I share a bath and an inside lavatory doesn't mean I'm not poor. Well, does it? I'm even unemployed. Oh, you think it's funny, but I am, I'm unemployed. My Father will leave nothing but debts, as Mama will tell you. He's left me what's left of his wine cellar, all his junk that nobody wants and he asked, yes he asked me last night, to leave all his empty champagne bottles to the Inland Revenue. Don't think he's got many of those even. I'll send mine for him. The kitchen's full.

CONSTANCE: I got the dustmen to take them away.

PAMELA: Well, please don't. They're for Father's Area Inspector. I promised him. Oh, I think about Vietnam. Not as much as you do. But I'm not giving my money away. Thank you. And then I think of myself. Don't you?

CONSTANCE: Yes. Pamela—

PAMELA: What? More?

CONSTANCE: Let me, let me try and help.

PAMELA: Help?

CONSTANCE: Yes.

PAMELA: What had you in mind?

CONSTANCE: You believe in friendship, don't you?

PAMELA: Yes.

CONSTANCE: Well. Let me do something. Was tonight bad?

PAMELA: Worse than yesterday. Oh, the same. The same. Could you close that window? I know you like fresh air, but this is ridiculous.

CONSTANCE: Sorry, I think your Mother—

PAMELA: Oh, of course. Yes, I believe in friendship, I believe in friendship, I believe in love. Just because I don't know how to doesn't mean I don't. I don't or can't. I wish she wouldn't call him Gideon. Oh, I suppose he doesn't mind. I do though. No, it's right for her to call him Gideon.

CONSTANCE: Isn't that what she always called him?

PAMELA: Yes. Well, it's his Christian name. Or one of his Christian names. His names are a bit of a mess, really. Well, his Father was a bit dotty and called him Tristram. Tristram, Gideon. Yes, well, you see, sort those out if

you're a lovely, struggling boy. And Papa thought of
Gideon and the Midianites, being brought up on the bible
and not much else, and liking earrings, I think it was the
earrings did it. He gave all his wives and mistresses and
girls, gave them all earrings. He gave me some. What do I
mean *some*? Have you seen my jewel-case? Oh, you must
see it. He was very good at women's jewellery. Well, what
was I saying? Oh, Gideon. Then, then there was his name,
his professional name. Prosser, Tristram Prosser, the old
boy must have been out of his mind, well, I think he was a
bit. He didn't want the old boy's name because he didn't
want to, to use the name even if it was a rotten one, *and*
Welsh one, mark. Because the old boy, *his* Father was a big
deal in the provinces. I mean he was so big in the
provinces he'd never come to London. Never came to
London in his life. Wasn't good enough for him. Conceited
old devil. So, anyway, Papa, when he started out of regard
for his Mother's agony in producing him—called
himself Orme. Passed the Square one day, small but
dignified he thought, that's it: Gideon Orme. Of course, he
was mad. But whoever knows about names? Gideon Orme.
Good God. I mean you couldn't get on the epilogue with a
name like that now. But then, well. . . . But people tried to
talk him out of it. I think it was trying to get away from
the Welsh and his Father and he got somehow stuck with
the Orme. He'd a Jewish grandmother. Always said that
was the best part of him. I doubt it but it might have
helped. But he used to say, I mean he never wanted *anyone*
to know about the *Prosser*, he'd say when the woodnotes go
really wild, my dear, it's just that keening old Welsh
self-regard. *Do* tell me. When I let it out. Pamela, if you
every hear me put the PEW into PURE, call out something
and something English and derisive or something because
then I'm being bad. And if I'm being bad. I'll go on
because no one will notice. They'll think it's just me. So
everyone called him Orme. I never called him anything
else. Not after Mama left. She *always* called him Gideon.
But in the profession he was just Orme. The Welsh are like

the Irish, he'd say they're too immodest to be really good actors. I don't want to be mistaken for one of these. Not that they'd know the difference. Except the Irish are a bit worse. Well, they invented the stage Irishman and blamed it on the English like everything else just to cover up. Dear Orme. He should be rescued from Andrew by now. He doesn't know how to abuse Andrew.

CONSTANCE: Haven't you told him?

PAMELA: He knows his ground with Edith. But with Andrew, he just doesn't know what he's about. You haven't met Andy, well, he's got none of Pauline's instinct to please, which is at least something, though not much. Mama thinks he's saint-like, and he probably is, except he's earth bound, he's saint-like, he's an opportunist, indulged, enclosed and supported by your colleague, his Father. What's *he* like?

CONSTANCE: I should say he's pretty able. Persuasive . . . quite attractive in some ways.

PAMELA: No, not him. Oh, then Daddy's brother saint character. Too good for politics. That's his badge.

CONSTANCE: Well—

PAMELA: He's too good to be true. That's why Mummy fell for him. He's not tough enough. For politics. And he's not good enough. Now, you're nearly tough enough but probably too good.

CONSTANCE: Thank you.

PAMELA: No, Andrew. Well, he started off as a wine snob.

CONSTANCE: Are you sure you won't?

PAMELA: Yes thanks.

CONSTANCE: I wish you'd talk to me.

PAMELA: What do you mean? I never stop talking to you. Why don't you tell me to shut up. I can go to bed, as you say.

CONSTANCE: No. Let's stay up a bit longer. I could do with an unwind myself.

PAMELA: What was *your* day like?

CONSTANCE: Busy. Bit end of term atmosphere.

PAMELA: Bit like a girls' school isn't it?

CONSTANCE: More like a boys' school where a few day-girls are tolerated.

PAMELA: I shouldn't have said you were ever tolerated. The place needs a bit of pash and glamour. You looked frightfully sexy in that pink dress, in the paper, you know meeting that delegation thing.

CONSTANCE: I don't think my constituents were too enthusiastic about it. They probably thought I didn't look serious enough.

PAMELA: You looked as if the entire Cabinet was lining up for you. They should be grateful you don't look like that woman—what is she, in the Treasury—the one with the teeth?

CONSTANCE: I wouldn't mind being as bright as she is.

PAMELA: I wouldn't mind if she were as pretty as you.

CONSTANCE: I don't think you should judge by externals so much.

PAMELA: I've just a superficial manner, often saying serious things. Which is the other way round to people like her. Just because she's got a double first in P.P.E. or I.T.V., there's no reason why she shouldn't get her teeth fixed. That's arrogance and self-deception. Perhaps that's why she's a big wheel in the Party.

CONSTANCE: I think she's a nice woman, really, shy and, yes, well a bit serious, but a first rate mind.

PAMELA: Um. Well, you know her. I find it hard to believe she's really wise to inflict those green teeth on people. Sort of autumnal teeth, aren't they? That should make her shy but she's not. I think someone must have told her once she looked like a tiger and she's been flashing them at you behind that crimped up seaweed she thinks is a serious politician's hair-do ever since. Is it a wig?

CONSTANCE: No. Poor woman. We can't all look like film stars.

PAMELA: Well, perhaps she should, poor dear. How can you be really intelligent and be satisfied with that? It's obviously all a great production number. Even if she does feel she's got unfair competition with the men

CONSTANCE: It isn't easy, Pamela. It's easier in your line.

PAMELA: Nonsense. Why do you have to strive? Besides, I don't look like a film star.

CONSTANCE: Yes, you do.

PAMELA: Yes, which one? It sure ain't Garbo. How old is she?

CONSTANCE: Garbo?

PAMELA: No, your lady.

CONSTANCE: Oh, thirty-seven, eight.

PAMELA: Well, she looks eighty-eight of course. Thirty-eight! You must be joking. Perhaps she should have the jabs, or a face job, or the lot. Perhaps she has already. Constance!

CONSTANCE: What?

PAMELA: Well—poor woman! Think! No wonder she's so solemn. Why, she's got tits like old ski-socks filled with sand. And a pre-form bra *no* one could make a wedge in. Is she married?

CONSTANCE: Oh, to some academic, I think.

PAMELA: Marriage must be pretty academic, too. Just as well.

CONSTANCE: I don't think you'd mind her so much if you met her. She's quite harmless.

PAMELA: You *can't* bring her back here—can you? To one of your parties? I know these brainy girls, they get terribly girlish and all frilly when you're not expecting it. They turn up at things like your Annual Conference Ball looking like Americans in cashmere sweaters with sequins on. And rhinestone spectacles. She's not harmless, she's not harmless at all. She's spending my money, and I haven't got any, you sit up there all hours of the night debating about how to spend my money. How to get hold of my money. What have you been doing with my money today? Give me those things, whatsit, Order Paper thing. What's this? Humber and Anglia Fisheries and Redevelopment Act. (*Pause*) And you won? Why don't you introduce the Lady Politicians' Teeth Filling Development Act? What's this?

CONSTANCE: Something I'm working on during the recess. Can I have it back, please? It's not interesting.

PAMELA: Then why are you working on it? "Striding into the Seventies with Labour!" You're really joking!

CONSTANCE: Please, Pamela. (*Pause.*)

PAMELA: Bit like school isn't it? Please can I have my satchel back? And then they throw it over the hedge for you. (*She*

32

gives it back.) Striding into the seventies. I haven't got used to hobbling about in the sixties yet. Give us a chance.

CONSTANCE: Time is in short supply in the present.

PAMELA: Then we should keep it in its place. Whenever we can. Just because we can't win.

CONSTANCE: It's very easy to poke at people who are trying to cope realistically with the future. And glib.

PAMELA: But what about the meantime? We've got to get through that, haven't we? I don't know about striding off anywhere. I seem to be stuck here for the moment . . . that's not being glib. We have to wait up . . . not be able to get to sleep . . . it's strange how easily men seem to get off to sleep . . . always before you . . . off . . . and you wake up tired . . . but not in the seventies . . . Tomorrow . . . that's early this morning, *this* morning. . . .

CONSTANCE: Why are you so scornful to me?

PAMELA: I'm not.

CONSTANCE: It's as if you hate what I do, what I am, everything about me. I know a lot of it seems funny and wasted effort but a lot of effort *is* funny and wasted.

PAMELA: I don't mind effort. I'm not so keen on strain.

CONSTANCE: You make me feel very shabby and inept and all thumbs sometimes.

PAMELA: *I* do! But, Constance, I don't . . . I don't know anything I'm ever talking about except for odd things. I'm almost totally ignorant, you know that.

CONSTANCE: No, you're not. You're very perceptive.

PAMELA: I'm not perceptive. I'm just full of bias. *And* I'm uneducated. I went to about twenty expensive schools and I never learnt anything in any of them. Except to play tennis.

CONSTANCE: You know how I admire you and what you do.

PAMELA: But I've never done anything very memorable. How can you?

CONSTANCE: I know you have formidable qualities . . .

PAMELA: Even if they haven't been exploited yet?

CONSTANCE: I respect and admire you for what you are.

PAMELA: I respect and admire you.

CONSTANCE: I don't think so. I wish you did.

PAMELA: It shouldn't matter to you.

CONSTANCE: Well, it does. Your good opinion is important to me. More so than most of the people I deal with. I know we inhabit different worlds, but they're not really so different always. And, also, I thought that we were, were very much alike you and I.

PAMELA: Yes. I always did too.

CONSTANCE: I couldn't believe it when you agreed to come and stay here.

PAMELA: Well: both left behind by our chaps. It gave us something to talk about in the long unconnubial nights.

CONSTANCE: I don't think it was as simple as that.

PAMELA: It wasn't so different moving out of my house. I didn't have much affection for it.

CONSTANCE: You wouldn't rather move back?

PAMELA: No. Are you suggesting it?

CONSTANCE: You know I'd like you to stay. But only if you want to. If I bore or irritate you—

PAMELA: Of course you don't, you idiot. We get on rather well, I think. You sounded like a wife then.

CONSTANCE: Did I? Sorry. It's just that I didn't want you to feel obliged to stay. You helped me over a difficult patch.

PAMELA: So did you. If I go back there, I only keep finding bits of his things in cupboards and drawers. Each time I think I have thrown everything out or sent it back to him, there's a belt or a tie or an old cheque book. I suppose I ought to let it. I just can't bring myself to all the bother of it.

CONSTANCE: I could find someone for you. It's not difficult to arrange. We always seemed to like the same things and react similarly. Most women just seem to make me impatient.

PAMELA: You prefer men. That's because you're such a gossip.

CONSTANCE: Really—I hate it.

PAMELA: Well, men are great on it.

CONSTANCE: But you know what I mean?

PAMELA: Yes. You like crowds too. So do men mostly. The sort you know.

CONSTANCE: What sort is that?

PAMELA: Oh, clever. Successful.

CONSTANCE: Do you know any unsuccessful men?

PAMELA: Well—not many maybe. But I know some pretty
stupid ones. Oh, darling, please don't look so upset. I'm
only chattering and going on about that poor lady's
rotten teeth. Everyone makes jokes about M.P.'s., they're
like honeymoon nights and mothers-in-law. Don't hold that
against me. I admire what you do tremendously. Just
because I haven't got the ability to do it myself.

CONSTANCE: You don't mean that.

PAMELA: But I do, my darling. It's like everyone thinks actors
have got no brains and live in some world walled up from
the realities everyone else is immersed in. Something. . . .

CONSTANCE: Your voice sounds quite different sometimes. I
suppose it's when you don't believe in the lines you're
reading.

PAMELA: How can I convince you?

CONSTANCE: You have.

PAMELA: Oh, for God's sake. Have some humour.

CONSTANCE: Please don't be angry. I'm sorry.

PAMELA: Sorry for what? Sticking up for yourself?

CONSTANCE: O.K. Let's not talk about it.

PAMELA: Well, why not talk about it? I've obviously upset you.

CONSTANCE: You didn't mean to.

PAMELA: Perhaps I did . . . I don't know. Maybe we should talk
about it.

CONSTANCE: Have some more of this. I'm glad you liked the
pink outfit. It was horribly expensive.

PAMELA: I could see. And don't change the subject. I don't think
I'm the only one who knows about clothes. I wish you
wouldn't buy cheap clothes.

CONSTANCE: Thanks.

PAMELA: Oh, hell, you know what I mean.

CONSTANCE: You just said it—I buy cheap clothes.

PAMELA: Well, it's all right for kids like Pauline.

CONSTANCE: She's young, you mean.

PAMELA: Yes, if you like. Who cares if she wears badly finished day to day rubbish, and if her skirts are up around her fat little thighs by her crutch.

CONSTANCE: We don't all have long legs like you.

PAMELA: But I wear them down to here.

CONSTANCE: Well? You have style.

PAMELA: So do you.

CONSTANCE: You don't think so.

PAMELA: How do you know? What I think? Nobody knows. I certainly don't at all.

CONSTANCE: Don't let's quarrel.

PAMELA: I thought we were having a parliamentary style debate on skirt length. Anyway, public opinion is on your side. They're not going below the knee for fifty years. I read it last night. (*Pause.*) Perhaps we aren't very alike after all, you and I?

CONSTANCE: Because we argue about skirt lengths?

PAMELA: I've thought about it lately. Orme was asking me about you tonight and I suppose it occurred to me then. I don't really think we are.

CONSTANCE: Probably.

PAMELA: You should be pleased. Not sad.

CONSTANCE: Perhaps I've always wanted to be someone like you. To have long legs, and style. Instead of just making efforts. But I suppose what's saddening is that you make it sound all like a rejection.

PAMELA: What?

CONSTANCE: Your attitude to me.

PAMELA: You make me sound like a selection committee that's turned you down.

CONSTANCE: I think you have.

PAMELA: Well, don't lose any sleep over it. I've turned down better people than you. (*Pause.*) I didn't mean that in the way it came out.

CONSTANCE: It probably came out purely enough. It seemed like it.

PAMELA: Why don't you make me shut up, go home. No, well go to bed, stop being a bitch.

CONSTANCE: I've told you: I like *you* as you are.

PAMELA: Well, you must be a pretty small club.

CONSTANCE: I really have made your teeth grate. I can see it.

PAMELA: You look so damned fragile sometimes. Someone should take you in his arms. Why doesn't that priggish, self-righteous husband come back and give you a cuddle or something. And own up he's been sleeping around himself for years and years!

CONSTANCE: He's got rigid standards. Besides, that's not what I need.

PAMELA: Oh, come off it, Constance, that's what we all need— love and friendship and a hot cuddle. And they really *are* on short supply.

CONSTANCE: It's very clear what your true opinion of me is. It's like the way some men look at one. Patting you on the head if you show signs of being bright, and picking you up and putting you down in *their* way—

PAMELA: Listen. You're far more likely to be bored by what you think of as my green room banter.

CONSTANCE: No. I think you're a very serious person. And I pay you the respect due to a serious person and what they do.

PAMELA: And what they do! That's it. You get this thing because you think I don't respect what you do. What you do, what you do, what you do, what's it matter? I don't care what anyone thinks.

CONSTANCE: I think you're lucky. At least you appear to. I'm afraid I *am* different.

PAMELA: My opinion about you or anything isn't worth—what —any more than that great booby of a tinker bell, Abigail! Abigail: just because she's made a movie and someone's talked about the mystery behind her eyes. She's got no mystery behind her eyes, she's just myopic which enables her to be more self-absorbed than ever and look as if she's acting when she's just staring at wrinkles on your forehead.

CONSTANCE: Thank heavens! Oh—come, there's more to her than that.

PAMELA: I'll tell you just what there is. And this I do know about. She moons about on street corners in a French movie, looks listless and beautiful in her own big, beady way while you hear a Mozart Requiem in the background. She plays with herself, gets the giggles while she's doing it and they say she's a cross between Garbo and Buster Keaton. Abigail—who's never seen a joke in her life when it was chalked on a blackboard for her, who was the only person in the entire world who didn't know the truth about her Daddy until she found him tucked up with a Greek cabin steward and the family's pet bulldog! And that was before she got engaged to the biggest poove in the business. She was *23*. And *20* already when she stood up to her nanny and told her she *would* go on dressing up as Castro if she wanted. to. I hope her movies are big in Cuba. They should be. They ask *her*, that blow-torch Mary Pickford what she thinks about the Russian and Chinese doctrinal conflict, and actually print what she says out of the hairy mystery behind her eyes.

CONSTANCE: That's better. You've stopped being cross with me.

PAMELA: Yes, I'm cross. What do you think she knows about it. She belongs to Disneyland. So do I. She doesn't even understand what's going on *there*. Except she knows she wants fat, sympathetic parts because she's dim enough to enjoy them and making sweeping, spurious gestures all over the place while she'll trample on a pussy cat or the char's baby to death while the world wonders how anyone can be so young, gifted, touching, and spirited and full of simple sorrow for the world's unloved and unwanted, while she herself is the most lovable and wanted of all starry creatures.

CONSTANCE: Hasn't she got a dress rehearsal for her play?

PAMELA: Yes. And she'll probably ring me if it's over and ask after dearest Orme. Not wondering whether or not I'm asleep. I know—I'm not. I'm talking about her. Give me some more of that. And silly actresses who don't know what they're talking about, and people like you bothering to listen to them.

CONSTANCE: Well, you're not Abigail.

PAMELA: No, I'm not. But if I were, I'd be what I'm not—a

whopping, enduring, ironclad, guaranteed star!

CONSTANCE: I think I'd better open another one. After Abigail.

PAMELA: Yes. If she rings, *you* talk to her. As for—are you all right now?

CONSTANCE: Fine. We both are. We *are* rather alike.

PAMELA: Maybe. Do you miss your child very much?

CONSTANCE: Yes.

PAMELA: How often do you see him?

CONSTANCE: About twice a week.

PAMELA: Do you mind *him* having custody. And all that meeting in the zoo and stuff?

CONSTANCE: I don't often enjoy it much.

PAMELA: What is he—four? I wouldn't mind having a son. Except I couldn't possibly look after it.

CONSTANCE: Of course you could. I think you'd be a lot of fun for a child.

PAMELA: Do you? I think I'd be easily bored. You have extraordinary belief in my abilities.

CONSTANCE: I don't think so. It's a little like feeling freshly looted each time.

PAMELA: Somebody loses. Somebody's guilty, somebody else comes through. When you win your constituency, the other poor candidate loses.

CONSTANCE: That's politics, He's a Tory.

PAMELA: So am I. I don't see why you should get on at my expense.

CONSTANCE: That's just an affectation.

PAMELA: No, it's not. I mean a real one. Not the sort you sit and make faces at. I couldn't afford a child in a property-owning democracy. I'd have to have loads of nannies. It could sit in the dressing-room sometimes—if I was working. But I'd have to be always working to pay for the nannies, and that wouldn't work at all.

CONSTANCE: You could get married.

PAMELA: What for?

CONSTANCE: It works for some people.

PAMELA: Tories like me are not "some people", Constance.

CONSTANCE: Some things do work you know.

PAMELA: You sound like Edith.

CONSTANCE: Thanks. I know what you think of her.

PAMELA: If I had a son, I wouldn't have a clue what I'd want him to be. I don't mean like an engine driver or something futile like an astronaut or a star export manager. I mean would he prefer champagne to drugs. I mean, I *wonder* about your child. Will he get stoned . . .

CONSTANCE: I believe the statistics suggest it's more likely than he's going to a university.

PAMELA: Oh, he'll go to a universty. If you've got "A" levels, we're after *you*! And even if you've only got "O" levels, we're *still* interested. Fancy. Lower streams of the poor little devils, upper levels of the bigger fish. I'd be in no stream at all. All those school inspectors and examiners and seducers from industry hanging about like men in raincoats, offering prospects and excitement and increments. How awful. If a man comes up to you, darling, however friendly he might be, talking about your "A" levels, don't, repeat don't, talk to him. He's after *you*, he wants to make a University Challenger out of you. Don't talk to them, they're sick. Yes, but Mummy's known it for a long time. Get back home before the park gates close or he'll take out his careers section in the Daily Telegraph and show it to you. Come home and you can have crumpets and champagne for tea with Mummy. Did you know that's the perfect device for testing whether your gynaecologist is any good or not? Do we drink champagne at bearing down time? Or do we not?

CONSTANCE: I wish I'd known.

PAMELA: My dear, first thing to ask. No, I don't really feel like you. I know, I don't, for instance, feel that most things I do must be an improvement on what I did before. So much improvement—like sex. I don't think I'm probably particularly good at it. I don't know. It's hard to tell, isn't it?

CONSTANCE: I think one knows pretty well. Well, at our stage of the game.

PAMELA: Yes. Perhaps you do have a more accurate notion.

You and Murray make it pretty big don't you?

CONSTANCE: Very.

PAMELA: Yes. I can see you do know.

CONSTANCE: I think you don't believe I know any more than you know.

PAMELA: Do stop reproaching me. With my late gentleman, it was pretty good I should say. *He* said it was. I suppose he was being truthful—as he saw it. However he saw it. Sometimes it was amusing. Or, of course, lonely. Or sometimes something not very much at all. That's not been your experience either much has it? Edith's always supposed to be great in the hay. Don't like to think about it. Least of all with Orme. *He* never spoke about it to me. But she's always telling me her ratty little details. She's not exactly fastidious. Now Orme. you could eat your dinner off his taste in anything. Constance: what's your other name?

CONSTANCE: Sophia. Female wisdom.

PAMELA: Oh my God, they lumbered you, didn't they? I'm not telling you mine. My Mother was really being pretentious. Pamela's bad enough. And *don't* tell me you like it. If you do, I'll tell you you don't have any style after all. (*Pause.*) Suppose it's trying to be honest to say you're not sure. (*At desk.*) "Going into Europe". Sounds like getting into the Pudding Club. Public spending, the price we have to pay, private sectors, incentive and exports, both—guess— both sides of industry, productivity, exploiting our resources to the full, readjustment. I suppose they're like words you're supposed to believe in, like your Catechism, I believe in God the Father, the Holy Catholic Church, forgive us our trade gaps.

CONSTANCE: I'm sorry, Pamela, I wish you wouldn't rummage around my desk. It's arranged very carefully.

PAMELA: So I see. I don't see, I mean I don't *see* economics at all. I mean I see astrology. Fine. But, well, ever since I have been born there's been an economic crisis. We went off something called the gold standard I think when I was born, there's been no confidence in sterling, crashes, devaluing, loans, and all the star gazing and at the end of

41

it people are better off, better fed, better housed than ever and if you never look at these forecasts, it makes no difference.

CONSTANCE: I think that's one of your simplifications, to put it mildly.

PAMELA: Would you? Say that would you? I'd say it was one of my commonplace revealed truths. However, you're the one who knows.

CONSTANCE: Oh, do stop saying that.

PAMELA: I don't think I've said it before. Did any letters come for me this morning?

CONSTANCE: No. I don't think so. Oh, a card from a gallery, I think. Any for me?

PAMELA: Don't know why I asked. No one every writes to me. Except for some occasional sun-questing queen who sends me a card from wherever the wog rumbo is thickest at the moment.

CONSTANCE: Was there any afternoon post, I asked you?

PAMELA: No, I don't think so. Some bills maybe.

CONSTANCE: Are you sure?

PAMELA: No. Why should you be in such a tizz about a few letters? Slow down.

CONSTANCE: I don't want to slow down if you mean come to a sort of standstill—

PAMELA: Implying?

CONSTANCE: It may seem inconsequential to you, but it *is* my work.

PAMELA: Not expecting a love letter. I thought Murray always rang.

CONSTANCE: No. He'll ring soon. I expect he's at a party.

PAMELA: Orme used to write beautiful letters. In superb handwriting, of course. He'd write to me regularly if he was on tour or in America. With little drawings, drawings of himself and what his mood was and what his performance looked like. He drew quite well. But he hasn't written to me for years. Not since he gave up work.

CONSTANCE: Why do people give up? I think I under-rate it.

PAMELA: I don't. I'm miserable when I'm not working, which is about half the time. You know what I'm like.

CONSTANCE: Well, then?

PAMELA: I think: excessive effort is vulgar.

CONSTANCE: Thanks again. Is that part of your high Toryism?
It's a little shopsoiled. That kind of romancing and
posturing I mean.

PAMELA: I think there's a certain grace in detachment.

CONSTANCE: You sound like an old-style lady journalist.

PAMELA: I thought you said saying "lady" anything was
condescending? That men did it to belittle women they saw
as rivals.

CONSTANCE: You never sound particularly detached. Your
onslaught on poor Abigail, for instance. Sounded just
vicious to me.

PAMELA: Ah, Constance, like so many people you don't
understand the content of tone of voice. You're like an
American, you have no ear. All voices are the same to you.
It's only what is said that seems significant. Old Orme *had*
to give up. What was there left for him? He'd done everything. He said I can't dodder on as Lear again. It needs a
younger man. Anyway, nobody liked it before when I did
it. Lost twenty thousand pounds. Said I was too young and
didn't care for the verse. You know how they say it as if
you ill-treated children. Now they'd say I was too old.
Mind you, I'd still be better than anyone else.

CONSTANCE: Must be great to have that degree of surety.

PAMELA: He just knew himself. And the others. He didn't want
to be liked particularly.

CONSTANCE: Lucky.

PAMELA: Essential if you're any good at all. He was cool.
Pauline and Dave think they're cool. But you can't be cool
if your sense of self and, well, ridicule is as numb as *theirs*.

CONSTANCE: Seems to me you're doing what you accuse me of—
theorizing.

PAMELA: True. Didn't somebody say "Addison in print was not
Addison in person"?

CONSTANCE: So? Miss Ignorant.

PAMELA: I think you *should* pay more attention to tones of

43

voice. They are very concrete. You have plenty of them.

CONSTANCE: You mean I dissemble?

PAMELA: I mean you are many things to different people.

CONSTANCE: A trimmer?

PAMELA: In the House, to your constituency, in the papers, on the telephone, in bed; I don't know about that, but you're determined not to be caught out. You're determined. You've read the books the others have, the reports, the things in the air at the moment, the present codes and ciphers. It all has to be broken down. The information has to be kept flowing. Or you'll feel cut off, left behind. You keep trying.

CONSTANCE: What should I do then?

PAMELA: What your fears and desires tell you together, I imagine. As you say, it's all stuff you enjoy. I tried writing love letters to someone. For quite a long time. Then I found my handwriting was getting like his. I don't know what I can go on saying. I love you. I need you. I want you. I ache for you. I need you beside me and in my bed. Don't let's part like this again. It's more than I can bear. It's never been like this in my life before. I never thought it could be. (*Pause.*) I tried writing erotica to him. But I couldn't bring myself to send it ever. I'd write it down, pages of it. I'd like to. I want you to . . . I dreamt that. . . . Then make up a dream. But it was too explicit. And then it seemed impersonal. Puritanism, I expect you'd say.

CONSTANCE: It's a pity you couldn't have gone with Murray to the party. He was frightfully sorry you couldn't go.

PAMELA: Was he? What did he think I'd do? Look in on my way from the hospital?

CONSTANCE: No, of course not. I think he just finds you very attractive. And it sounded as if there might be some interesting people there.

PAMELA: I've been meeting interesting people for years. I just wish people would stop trying to fix you up. So and so would like to meet you. Just scalps. I'm thirty four . . . twenty six years old, and I don't need to go to parties and meet interesting people. I can make out for myself even if

44

the terrain *is* all married men, pooves and tarted up
heteros head over heels about themselves.

CONSTANCE: Like your friend Edward?

PAMELA: He's not my friend or my lover or anything. He just
comes in and talks to me. I suppose even he gets bored
with his dollies and scrubbers. Not with himself, mind, but
he can't believe that there's someone who doesn't think
he's the greatest knock-out a woman ever laid eyes on.

CONSTANCE: Why should it bother him?

PAMELA: Good question. He's younger than I am—though not
as much as he says. I know that. He's a big deal star and a
new scene and all that. As for Murray, he's *your* gentleman.

CONSTANCE: He's intrigued by you.

PAMELA: Well, he shouldn't be telling you then. It's unfair and
unkind. What's the matter with him?

CONSTANCE: He doesn't. I've watched him look at you. And
sometimes I know he's thinking of you.

PAMELA: He hardly knows me.

CONSTANCE: He knows you through me.

PAMELA: That's scarcely the same.

CONSTANCE: It's quite potent.

(*Phone rings.*)

I'll take it.

PAMELA: Why are you always so sure it must be for you? It's
probably some man sniffing around. The moment you've
been detached, they're on the doorstep seeing what the
chances are.

Especially for you—married women on the shelf. Wanting
to be taken down and given a bit of what they need.

CONSTANCE: It's probably Murray.

PAMELA: If it's Lady Tinker-Bell Abigail, I'm in bed.

CONSTANCE (*phone*): Hello . . . Oh yes, just a minute. . . . It's
Andrew.

PAMELA: Hello. . . . Yes. I *am* in bed. You've woken me up. . . .
Well, your Mama may send him to sleep. . . . What time?
. . . No, all right. . . . Well, I'll just have to manage, won't
I? Yes, I know you have to work. . . . What *are* you doing?
Good God. Oh well—what's all that noise? I see. . . . Night.

CONSTANCE: Nothing wrong?

PAMELA: Oh, he wants to leave the hospital earlier to get to work.

CONSTANCE: We shouldn't bicker. Please forgive me. I know what it must be like for you.

PAMELA: We're not quarrelling are we?

CONSTANCE: Well, I think we're a bit out of kilter.

PAMELA: Do you know where he is? Andrew? He's just left Orme and gone to that party. I suppose he's one of the interesting people. What's the betting Edward isn't there too? He told me to tell you your gentleman's just leaving.

CONSTANCE: I didn't know he knew Murray.

PAMELA: Well, they know each other now. Lucky Murray. I wonder what other celebrities he's met.

CONSTANCE: It sounded rather more a literary-political sort of do.

PAMELA: Oh, I think Andrew's got literary connections of a kind.

CONSTANCE: What's he do?

PAMELA: At present? Seems he's a waiter in one of the fag amateur restaurants in Brompton Road. Dressed as a lion tamer, I think.

CONSTANCE: Perhaps we should go? Murray adores those sort of places.

PAMELA: Not if you're hungry.

CONSTANCE: Do they let girls in the place? Or just tamper with their food?

PAMELA: The food doesn't go to much tampering. He's a poet. I think he cuts out bits of old copies of the Illustrated London News and American comics and pastes them together. Yes, they get published. He used to paint a little in the same fashion. He'd glue bits of his levis on to strips of glass and top them up with different coloured paints and plaster. He told me this evening he wants his Dad to put him into publishing. Perhaps that's why he went to Murray's party. He's very keen on a lot of American plays, sort of about leaving nude girls in plastic bags at railway stations. Non verbal, you understand, no old words, just

the maximum in participation. I don't know whether the
the old boy will stump up. Perhaps Murray could help him.
CONSTANCE: Why should he?
PAMELA: I don't know. A lot of people find him "interesting".
Some weekends he runs old movies backwards on the
ceiling in an old Bethesda chapel in Holland Park.
(*Door bell.* CONSTANCE *rushes to it.* MURRAY *is there. Thirtyish.*)
CONSTANCE: Darling!
MURRAY: Get my message?
CONSTANCE: Yes. Come in.
MURRAY: Am I too late?
CONSTANCE: No. We're just having some champagne.
PAMELA: Have some.
MURRAY: Thanks. How are you, Pamela?
PAMELA: Not bad.
CONSTANCE: She's exhausted, poor darling. Make her go to bed.
I can't.
MURRAY: You look remarkable for it.
CONSTANCE (*to* PAMELA): See?
PAMELA: See what?
MURRAY: How's your Father?
PAMELA: Oh. The same. As far as I know.
MURRAY: I'm sorry. I just met your brother.
PAMELA: Please—*step*-brother.
CONSTANCE: Sit down, darling. Doesn't he look smashing?
PAMELA: Ravishing. How was the party?
MURRAY: Not bad. Heard one or two interesting things. What
does your step-brother do?
PAMELA: Now? He's a part-time pouve's waiter.
MURRAY: He told me he was going into publishing.
PAMELA: I expect he will. He started off as a wine snob, going
to vineyards and reporting on growth and so on. It was for
this City firm and he used to dress like an old Etonian then.
Before that he was at one of Mama's pet schools and wore
levis and wax in his ears like pearl earrings. Same at the
university.
MURRAY: Which one?
PAMELA: Oh, I don't know, one of those new estates where all

the furniture looks to have come from Heals' January sales. He became a probation officer for a bit. He'd a degree for that kind of service. He wanted to do something 'meaningful' as my American gentleman used to say. He got accused of having relations with a boy from an approved school. Anyway, they thought he'd got the wrong meaning and I think he was bored and underpaid, so he did do Zen for a bit but I don't think he got paid for it. Then the Committee of 100. He's always been pretty violent so he enjoyed hitting his great head against brutal bobbies for a spell. Oh, and he went to Cuba. Same time as Lady Tinker-Bell the blow torch.

MURRAY: Lady Tinker-Bell?

CONSTANCE: She means Abigail.

MURRAY: Do I detect professional envy?

PAMELA: Professional boredom. He'd send me cards and pictures of Abigail in her Castro hat singing people's songs. But he got some Cuban girl in the pudding club and got knifed by a fellow revolutionary, so perhaps he wasn't bent after all. Anyway, he got slung out for bourgeois carryings-on.

MURRAY: You're not exaggerating of course?

PAMELA: Murray, I *never* exaggerate. You're like your Constance. No ear for inflection.

MURRAY: He seemed pretty lively to me.

PAMELA: Did he? Yes, I suppose he did. He'd been cooped up in quite the wrong scene all the evening. What's the matter? You think I'm frivolous?

MURRAY: I don't know you.

PAMELA: Constance says you do.

CONSTANCE: She's no more frivolous than I am.

PAMELA: No? I think Murray's one of those intellectuals who thinks all actors live in a narrow, insubstantial world, cut off from the rest of you. Well, kid yourself not. You're all of you in Show-Business now. Everybody. Of course, Orme was never in Show-Business. Books, politics, journalism, you're all banging the drum, all performers now. What are you busying yourself with these days?

MURRAY: Oh, usual stuff. Reviewing, articles, bits on the box.

48

CONSTANCE: He's written a play. I think it's quite extraordinary. Tell her about it.

MURRAY: If you'd like me to.

PAMELA: No. I can't bear people describing things like that to me. The people who do it well are usually no good anyway. They're just critics passing as writers.

CONSTANCE: Then you must read it. Really.

PAMELA: All right, Constance. But don't sell it to me.

(*Phone rings.*)

PAMELA: Yours, I suppose.

(CONSTANCE *has got to it.*)

CONSTANCE: Yes . . . Abigail?

PAMELA: I'm asleep. No thanks to her.

CONSTANCE: I made her go to bed. She's worn out, poor dear . . . Yes, nearly all day . . . No different I'm afraid.

PAMELA: As if she cares. Get rid of her.

CONSTANCE: Yes, I'll tell her . . .

PAMELA: No, don't.

CONSTANCE: How was your dress rehearsal? . . . How exciting for you. . . .

PAMELA: I'll bet.

CONSTANCE: And now you go on tour first? Well, I hope it goes well. . .

PAMELA: Oh, it will. A bomb in Brighton. They should burn that joint down. They think it's 1950.

CONSTANCE: I'll give it to her. . . .

PAMELA: Tell her to get her girdle washed.

CONSTANCE: Of course, we'll come. . . .

PAMELA: No, she doesn't wear underwear, lovely.

CONSTANCE: Yes, we'll come round after. If you'd like us to. . . .

PAMELA: Isn't there a touring date in Vietnam?

CONSTANCE: No, I was up, anyway. . . . 'Bye. . . .

PAMELA: Well done.

CONSTANCE: I could hardly be rude to her could I? I don't know her.

(*Door bell.*)

PAMELA: Oh, God, open house! I *will* go to bed.

MURRAY: I'm sorry—

PAMELA: No. Not you.

(CONSTANCE *goes to the door.* EDWARD *is there. Looks about twenty-eight.*)

PAMELA: What do you want?

CONSTANCE: Edward.

EDWARD: Sorry. I saw your light.

PAMELA: No, you didn't. You just rang. Why don't you knock up Abigail in the middle of the night. She likes pure, spontaneous gestures.

EDWARD: I just left her. I went to her dress rehearsal.

CONSTANCE: Come in then. Have a drink. You know Murray.

EDWARD: Hi.

MURRAY: How was it? The dress rehearsal.

EDWARD: Oh, O.K. I was in the bar in the middle act with some of the kids.

PAMELA: Fine.

EDWARD: I guess it was all right. I just think plays are a bit of a drag.

CONSTANCE: Didn't you do one last year?

EDWARD: Yeah. But six weeks was all I could take. And I had to fire the director and keep fighting to keep the author out and all that jazz.

PAMELA: That and never knowing his lines and getting drunk and not turning up twice a week.

EDWARD: We broke the house record.

PAMELA: You're a big star, darling. One epic in two and a half years and a nose job.

EDWARD: Am I in the way?

CONSTANCE: Not at all.

PAMELA: Would you mind?

CONSTANCE: We can't get Pamela to go to bed.

EDWARD: No. Well, it's early.

PAMELA: Why aren't you out hell-raising or whatever you do in the newspapers.

EDWARD: Things are pretty quiet. Don't know where everybody is.

PAMELA: London's full of interesting people, especially for you

50

Edward. I don't know why you're called a hell raiser—it's
only getting drunk all night—that and working at being
louder and more Welsh than even you are—and you've got
a very poor head. No dollies tonight?

EDWARD: Well, Sue's at home. But I thought I'd look around.

PAMELA: Sue won't take that so well. She likes to go out with
you. She's like the old line about justice—not only must be
done but must be seen to be done. Why don't you two go
to bed?

CONSTANCE: What about you?

PAMELA: I'm coming. I'll put the lights out and get rid of
Edward.

EDWARD: Any brandy in the house?

CONSTANCE: Sure. Murray? How about you?

MURRAY: All right. I'll take one to bed with me.

CONSTANCE: Please don't keep her up, Edward. She's flaked out.

EDWARD: Right. (*Helping himself.*)

MURRAY: Goodnight, Pamela; I hope your Father's better.

PAMELA: Thanks.

CONSTANCE: Don't forget. If you want *anything* tomorrow. I'm
so sorry about tonight.

PAMELA: *I'm* sorry.

(CONSTANCE *embraces her.* MURRAY *watches.*)

CONSTANCE: Goodnight, Edward.

EDWARD: 'Night.

(MURRAY *and* CONSTANCE *go into bedroom.*)

EDWARD: Big thing going?

PAMELA: I imagine so.

EDWARD: Things same at the hospital then?

PAMELA: Yes. Sorry to be rude, Edward. But you should know
by now. You're thirty-four, even if you do say you're
thirty-one.

EDWARD: How do you know?

PAMELA: I always know these things. I will go to bed in a
minute so let yourself out when you've finished will you?

EDWARD: Sure.

PAMELA: Why don't you go back to your famous bachelor pad.
Sue'll be in a state if she doesn't know where you are.

51

EDWARD: I'll let myself out.

PAMELA: You ring her and say you're on your way if you like. Shall I?

EDWARD: You know, Pam, I've always thought you were a very sexy kid.

PAMELA: You told me the other week for about five hours. Well, I'm rather disappointing I believe, and I'm twenty-six and I'm no kid.

EDWARD: You're not twenty-six but you've got a lot going. I never saw Orme in Macbeth. What was he like?

PAMELA: The best.

EDWARD: So they tell me. Bit before my time.

PAMELA: Too bored to bother, you mean.

(*He picks up cuttings book.*)

EDWARD: Here he is. Playing Arthur Bellenden. Of the 21st London Regiment. Act One. Nutley Towers. A Friday Evening. He looks quite something.

PAMELA: He was—he was ravishing.

EDWARD: Act II. The Conservatory Nutley. Sunday Evening. Act III. The Marskby Drawing Room. Fitzroy Square. Monday Evening. What's it called?

PAMELA: "The Call of Duty".

EDWARD: Good stuff. Orchestra under the direction of Mr. Reginald Garston. What's this entracte?

PAMELA: Quite ravishing.

EDWARD: Shaftesbury Theatre, May 7th, 1922. Here's a good one. "The Undecided Adventuress". Wonder what she couldn't decide.

PAMELA: Mary or a life of sin. Great long thighs.

EDWARD: "Master, you owe on the firm £7,000. If it's not deposited in the company's bank by midday on Monday, you shall have to face up to the dishonour. Your rank is nothing to me. I will brook no arguments, no entreaties. Not even for the sake of Effie." Effie! "You have brought disgrace enough on her already." I'm sorry. I didn't mean anything.

PAMELA: Why not try Abigail again?

EDWARD: She's tired.

PAMELA: Tired. I'm sure she'd accommodate *you* if you persist.
EDWARD: She's not all that great at it, anyway.
    (*Phone rings.*)
EDWARD: Don't worry. I'll go. Shall I take it?
    (*She nods. He takes phone.*)
EDWARD: Yeah . . . Hang on . . . Pauline.
    (PAMELA *goes.*)
PAMELA: What is it? I'm asleep. I'm asleep. I'm trying to stay
    asleep. . . . When? Why didn't you ring before . . . I could
    have come then. . . . No, I'll come down later . . . I've
    taken a pill. Oh, Mother can make all the arrangements.
    She'll enjoy all that. . . . No, don't put her on. . . . Hello.
    . . . No, well, I mistimed it didn't I? . . . Please don't get
    hysterical *now*, it's bad timing. . . . No, I can't. . . . Get
    Andrew . . . get Andrew to come down. . . . Yes. . . .
    Later. (*She puts the phone down.*)
EDWARD: Pamela. I'm so sorry. I suppose you're not surprised.
    Can I get you a drink?
PAMELA: There's one more bottle of champagne in the fridge
    (EDWARD *goes to get it. She looks at the open cuttings book,*
    while he opens the fresh bottle.)
    "A Weekend Gentleman". He was a vile seducer in that.
    "And your unborn child. You shall never see it, Gerald.
    I shall see to it that it grows up in sweetness and ignorance,
    far, far away from where your guilty hands can ever find
    her". Sounds like a paedophiliac or whatever.
EDWARD: What's that?
PAMELA: Someone who likes children. No, he wouldn't have
    played that. He would have thought it most improper.
    Besides, it would have made him giggle. He was a terrible
    giggler. He must have been the other man. They didn't like
    him to be a rotter. When he was, he was a frightful flop.
    And he giggled too much. (*She raises her freshly filled*
    champagne glass.) Oh, Orme. . . . Orme . . . my darling. . . .
EDWARD: Shall I stay a little?
PAMELA: If you like. We can finish this together.

CURTAIN.

ACT TWO

Same scene. Some weeks later. PAMELA *is in a nightdress and dressing gown. It is late afternoon. She is drinking a glass of champagne. In the room are* EDITH *and* PAULINE. EDITH *is rather formally dressed. Even* PAULINE *is slightly subdued.*

EDITH: I still think you should have come.

PAMELA: So you said.

EDITH: There were quite a lot of people there. After all, when you think he hadn't been on the stage for about ten years. And a whole generation have hardly even heard of him.

PAMELA: You sound as if you're surprised there was anyone there. After all, you're the one responsible for the thing happening. Orme would have hated the idea. I don't think he ever went to a memorial service in his life. He'd have laughed his head off at the idea, rows of his friends having to listen to Handel and Wesley and knighted actors reading the lesson. He'd have thought it very common.

EDITH: I don't think he'd have said that.

PAMELA: Well, it wasn't for me. It was for Orme.

EDITH: I saw Constance there.

PAMELA: Well, she likes a good blub. It's like singing the Red Flag to her.

EDITH: And that man in the opposition Front Bench. The one who's so hot on the arts. You always see him at Covent Garden.

PAMELA: Can't think. Tory poove I suppose.

EDITH: After all, he *was* knighted himself. He can't have been that aloof.

PAMELA: Mama: only because he knew you wanted it so much. Which is why he kept turning it down until after you'd broken up.

EDITH: I hope that's not true. It sounds very petty. And if it is true, it isn't kind to point it out.

54

PAMELA: Wit very often is petty, Mama, and, knowing him, I
can't honestly believe it hadn't occurred to him. I told him
it was petty myself. And rather common. However, he
didn't make too many mistakes. And today's circus he
can't be held responsible for. That's your fault.

EDITH: In that case, there may be a certain ironic justice in it.

PAMELA: You really didn't like him did you? How's the
bookshop, Pauline?

PAULINE: Oh, I goofed over that. I went broke in two weeks.
Don't know why. Business was fine. Management I guess.
That's what Dave thinks.

EDITH: Have you been out, Pamela?

PAMELA: Out?

EDITH: Since the funeral. You never seem to answer the
telephone.

PAMELA: I take sleeping pills during the day and turn off the
telephone. Constance doesn't like it. I think she's terrified
the Prime Minister will ring up and there's no one to take
the message. She's getting an answering service.

EDITH: Very wise. I should think you must be losing offers,
don't you?

PAMELA: Work? I shouldn't think so.

EDITH: I mean people will probably think of you at the moment.

PAMELA: People never think of me as Orme's daughter. There's
too much space between us. Besides, you don't get offered
work like compassionate leave. They leave you alone.
They'd rather. It only reminds them. So what are you
doing, Pauline? Changing your scene then?

PAULINE: Yes. Dave and I thought we'd try the sun for a bit.

PAMELA: Oh, yes, I've had offers of going to the sun. It's a little
like when your chap has left you. They suddenly remember
you and see if you're on top again.

PAULINE: Oh, Spain. Somewhere. . . .

EDITH: But you'll need to work again soon, won't you? You
haven't done anything for ages.

PAMELA: That's right.

EDITH: I mean you do know Gideon's left hardly anything
except a few debts and mementoes, which he seems to have

55

left mostly to you.

PAMELA: They're not worth much. He had a comfortable retirement.

EDITH: Don't you think you ought to be looking? Seriously?

PAMELA: Don't worry, Mama. I shan't come to you for anything.

EDITH: Isn't your agent, Bernard whatsaname doing anything for you?

PAMELA: If there's anything, he'll come and knock the door down and wake me up. I think the time comes when you no longer follow the sun. Orme and I used to go to the west coast of Scotland—at least we did a couple of years running. I'm rather bored with my useless golden body. It's had thousands lavished on it in air fares and sun oil and hundreds of broiler bikinis. I think I shall use a sunshade. I'm tired of juggling face down with my bra straps and all that. I think a sun tan is definitely vulgar. It's like dieting. *That's* vulgar. It's just uncollected effort.

PAULINE: You're lucky.

PAMELA: No, I'm fastidious, fortunately I don't like rich food. And I don't like getting drunk in a certain way. That's vulgar. You and Dave both diet, don't you? I'm not surprised. He's far too fat for a man of his age. What is he—twelve? He eats too much and drinks too much. You can't eat *and* drink. One or the other. Orme drank. Better for you. If you drink the right thing.

PAULINE: Dave doesn't drink.

PAMELA: Well, sitting around smoking pot in groups is vulgar. So are nervous breakdowns. Meretricious. I've had at least three. I lay in them like I used to water ski and play tennis. Like I made love at your age, With those acrobatic, expert wogs in Milan and Paris. Mind you, I always *used* people like ski-instructors. I promised them nothing and gave them nothing. Instructors. Like theatre directors. Only faggots and middle-aged women in books written by faggots have affairs with ski-instructors.

EDITH: But what are you going to do, Pamela?

PAMELA: I told you. I shall probably take my sunshade to the

South of France for a week or two. It's warm and I can
drink champagne and swim. I like to swim still. And I can
usually avoid anyone I know. I'll wear a black armband.
I've got a couple of nice new frocks that will go very well
with it.

EDITH: You don't have any work, any aim, hardly any friends
now, except for a few—

PAMELA: Homosexuals? Well, they've mostly given me up. I'm
ultimately unrewarding to them. Which is just as well.
Except for Bernard of course. If you're a woman or a moll,
you do have to spend quite a lot of energy flattering them
with your sympathy and admiration and performing like
captured prize dogs for them. I think Bernard's different.
But they do conform to their archetype. Like most sizeable
pressure groups, I suppose, and not even poor liberal
Constance can really escape the fact, beyond all her
Parliamentary recommendations, that as a group they *are*
uniformly bitchy, envious, self-seeking, fickle and usually
without passion.

EDITH: You do generalise, Pamela.

PAMELA: Mama, if you've never had the discomfort of having
what are commonly known as crabs—which I know you
haven't—do listen to someone who has suffered from them
constantly. Even Bernard agrees with me. In fact, I think
he said it to me.

PAULINE: Is Constance going to marry that guy?

PAMELA: I expect so. Yes, I expect I shall have to change my
scene. Constance is very accomplished. She can cook every
sort of cooking, write books, give you an opinion on
anything from Marxist criticism of the novel to Godard,
she's even managed to get herself a child, an ex-husband
and now a well thought-of lover.

EDITH: Perhaps you should try writing a book. You could do a
biography of Gideon. Who could be better?

PAMELA: Not me. He wouldn't want it either.

EDITH: Or a novel. Look at the people you've met in the past
ten years or so, not just in your own line.

PAMELA: You're like Constance.

EDITH: Well, she's right. You don't look at all well. Staying indoors, sleeping all day for weeks on end, living on champagne. Which you can't afford.

PAMELA: One of the several reasons I am getting out of here is that I fancy Constance is going to write a book with me in it. You should always beware of lady writers. They hover and dart about like preying fish in a tank. They've their eyes on you and little tape recorders whining away behind their ears by way of breathing apparatus. Then they swallow you up whole and spew you up later, dead and distorted. Nothing has happened to you in the mean-time except that they turn you into waste material. Because the trouble with lady writers is they've usually no digestive juices. They're often even surprised you're not pleased. There, I gobbled you up whole. Aren't I swift, don't I move, don't I watch. Like hell you do. You just can't deal with it decently once you've got it. That friend of yours—oh, Mildred—that one did it to *me* once.

EDITH: I didn't think she meant it was you.

PAMELA: She wasn't sure whether to be pleased when people recognised me, or to just pass it off as her own inventive craft.

EDITH: I can't remember.

PAMELA: She even described me physically—she's a mess herself of course. Then a quick run down on my character and finished up patronizing me for being less intellectually perceptive, and so ending up as a puppet—and I mean puppet—in her clever dickdyke thirty bobs worth, and not being similarly bright enough to write a book about her and the mess *she* is.

EDITH: You're not being fair to Mildred. She's got quite a reputation.

PAMELA: She has.

EDITH: You're unfair to everyone. Including yourself.

PAMELA: I hope so. Help. You've seen I'm still around, Mama, why don't you get back. Your old man must be worried about you.

EDITH: I'm concerned about you Pamela.

PAMELA: Well, don't be. We've managed quite well without each other for about twenty years.

EDITH: It's not been easy.

PAMELA: I couldn't have changed it.

EDITH: What's going to happen to you?

PAMELA: I shall go on as I have done for twenty nine years.

EDITH: As you say, you've never married or had children. Well, that's all right, there's no reason why you should if you don't feel the need to. At least people are beginning to realise a woman isn't a freak if she wants other things out of life. But there *are* other things, like work, yes and having affairs and even making love. You can't want to stop all that at your age. You're young and intelligent and healthy and attractive. And a lot of people like you. Constance adores you. She says lots of people do and you aren't always aware of it.

PAMELA: Constance sometimes has her ear to the ground of the wrong building.

EDITH: You seem to have no impulse about these things, or even ordinary things like whether to move or take a holiday, go out or sit in the sun. I know you're upset about Gideon but you'd been like this for a long time before.

PAMELA: I shall manage within my own, my own walls. I've no ambitions. I've told you: I love acting. I'm not so keen on rehearsals. I don't wish to be judged or categorized or watched. I don't want to be pronounced upon or do it for anyone.

EDITH: Will you go back to your house?

PAMELA: I suppose so. At least it's mine.

EDITH: Won't it seem strange without a man about the house.

PAMELA: Really! Edith. No, it won't seem strange at all. (*Phone rings.*) Answer it, will you? I'm out.

PAULINE: Hello. . . . Just a minute, I'll see. . . . It's your agent, Bernard. I thought you'd want to. . . .

EDITH: We'd better go,

PAMELA: It's nothing you can't hear. (*On phone.*) Darling! How nice . . . Oh, I'm all right . . Yes, really . . . Well, I've not been answering the phone . . . Well, I'm glad you didn't . . .

I couldn't afford to get the door fixed . . . Oh, you went?
. . . No . . . I know Orme wouldn't have gone for it . . .
What made you go? . . . Oh, well I'm glad you enjoyed it
. . . It seems to have been a success. I thought it was all
frightfully respectable. Who let you in, you great Jewish
queen? . . . Oh don't you start "what's your scening" me,
baby! Well, you're a very mutton old hippy dressed up as
lamb! And how are things for you? What a love life you do
have . . . How do you find the time? No, I'm twenty nine
this week. Period of mourning has aged me for a bit. Till
next week . . . You must tell me all about it . . . Yes, all
the details . . . you know I must have them . . . I'll tell
you . . . what . . . nothing . . . only my stepmother . . . yes,
and my little stepsister . . . oh, years younger . . . can't you
hear her shaking her cannabis rattle?
(*Enter* MURRAY *front door. She motions him in.*)
All right, listen, Bernie . . . you know that address book
of yours. The one with names of the gentlemen in it. Yes,
Ladies Services. Can you give me a few numbers and which
names to mention when I ring? . . . No, of course I'm not,
darling. After all this time . . . Yes, for a little friend . . .
All right, ring me back. But don't leave it . . . Yes, well it
is urgent. It always is, isn't it . . . Oh, and I'm changing
my address. No, not scene, I'm going back to my house . . .
Yes, of course, I'm all right . . . Right . . . soon now,
mind . . . Hello, Murray. You know my mother and
stepsister, Pauline.

MURRAY: How do you do.

EDITH: We'd better go. Do try and answer the phone. And let
me know when you go back to the house. And try to get
something to eat.

MURRAY: I'll see she gets something.

EDITH: I wish you would. Thank you.

MURRAY: Goodbye, Mrs— . . .

(*Nobody helps.* EDITH *goes to kiss* PAMELA.)

PAMELA: I haven't cleaned my teeth Mama. (*She lights a
cigarette.*) I'll give you a ring.

(*The other two* WOMEN *go out.*)

You needn't bother to follow up that offer,

MURRAY: Are you sure?

PAMELA: Quite.

MURRAY: Do you think you should be drinking that?

PAMELA: Certainly. It's very good. My agent sent it round as a present. I think he must spend all his commission on it for me. I pay him ten per cent and I seem to get it back in crates.

MURRAY: Was that who you were talking to?

PAMELA: He'd been to Orme's Memorial. He can't resist that sort of thing.

MURRAY: Connie went. I couldn't manage it.

PAMELA: She couldn't resist it either. I saw her all dressed up for it this morning. I went back to sleep.

MURRAY: What was, was that about Ladies' Services?

PAMELA: None of your business. Have some of this.

MURRAY: It is.

PAMELA: It was a private telephone conversation.

MURRAY: I can't pretend I didn't hear it. Come on. What are Ladies' Services?

PAMELA: What do you suppose?

MURRAY: Pamela?

PAMELA: What are you doing here?

MURRAY: Don't be pompous suddenly. I came to see you.

PAMELA: Constance will be here soon. She's only gone to a meeting. It was after Orme's do. I wish you'd go away. This, of course is the, I mean, this is it, the disadvantage, this is why you shouldn't, this is sharing with, with, yes, look, Murray, don't stand there just arrived, I don't need anything, yes I'm in the club, everything's in control, I'm sitting here with a drink, I've got the telephone, I've got friends, I like you quite a lot, but I'd like some, oh, privacy, I guess. Anyway, I'd like to be alone, and not stared at, please go away, ring up Constance, no, waylay her outside and take her to a movie in Westbourne Grove or something. Things . . . are very . . . easy.

MURRAY: Oh, Pamela, what's happened to us?

PAMELA: Don't "oh Pamela" like that. You're another Constance. We *aren't* alike. Nothing much has happened.

61

I'm getting out this evening. My Mama decided me.

MURRAY: You mustn't do that.

PAMELA: I'm not getting out of anything that's necessarily happened. I'm just getting back to where I used to live, such as it was. Not very much. But I can warm it up after a day or two.

MURRAY: I'm going to tell Connie, I don't care what you say.

PAMELA: Do what you like. If you do, you're more feeble than I thought.

MURRAY: You think I'm feeble then?

PAMELA: Oh, yes. Don't you?

MURRAY: What do you mean?

PAMELA: You just want to be spoilt and cossetted because you've convinced Constance and I suppose others I don't know about that there's something special about you. What it is I don't know.

MURRAY: And *you* don't want spoiling?

PAMELA: No. And you couldn't do it, anyway.

MURRAY: We could do all sorts of things.

PAMELA: Like?

MURRAY: Like, for instance . . .

PAMELA: Spare me a list . . .

MURRAY: What do you mean: feeble?

PAMELA: Immature, I suppose.

MURRAY: That's what women usually say about men when they can't keep up with them.

PAMELA: I dare say. We don't match up, you see.

MURRAY: What are you going to do?

PAMELA: I wish everyone would just stop asking me: what am I going to do. I am going to get up and I am going to go to sleep, if I've got enough to knock me out. I'm going to speak to Bernard and get his list of Ladies' Services.

MURRAY: And then what?

PAMELA: I shall go back to my little house and one day I shall pick up the telephone when it rings. And if it doesn't ring, never mind. I may have to ring someone else instead. If they're in . . .

MURRAY: I shall come round to the house.

PAMELA: Oh, for God's sake.

MURRAY: I mean it.

PAMELA: Then I suppose I'll have to go and stay with Bernard. He'll look after me and he'll get the police on to you. He'll enjoy that.

MURRAY: I do love you.

PAMELA: Well, even if you do . . .

MURRAY: What is it?

PAMELA: What is what?

MURRAY: Haven't you got anything to say to me?

PAMELA: No, Murray. Not really. We've had a good time together, because we've hardly been together—

MURRAY: We could be . . .

PAMELA: Well, we won't be . . .

MURRAY: Why not?

PAMELA: My nose says so.

MURRAY: Mine says the opposite.

PAMELA: Well, I rely on mine. Not yours. But, anyway, it's had its pleasure. Don't renounce them. I've been looking at Abigail's notices. Before my Mama and little sister arrived.

MURRAY: You want me to stay with Connie?

PAMELA: No.

MURRAY: Well?

PAMELA: You will find each other. Or not. I don't want to talk about it. I won't be involved in your life, or hers. I'm sorry for both of you. *Not* much. A bit. You'll manage, so shall we all. Just remember: what I should do now or at any time is nothing to do with either of you. I owe you no confidence.

MURRAY: Pamela, let's talk about it.

PAMELA: You always want to talk about it. I don't want to, I'm not going to. Now go or talk about something else. Anyway, I'm getting dressed. And I don't like being watched.

MURRAY: You'll change your mind. You will. There's always time for that. I know the handling of you. I really do.

PAMELA: Good. Like a horse. Did you go to Abigail's play? Oh yes, you went with Constance. She didn't seem to to like it much. Did you?

MURRAY: Quite. She seemed to enjoy it to me.

PAMELA: Ah! She said it was really about a sort of regional mysticism that didn't, or couldn't, er, engage her, oh, attention, her full interest.

MURRAY: I don't think the play was really about regional mysticism. Whatever that . . .

PAMELA: Indeed?

MURRAY: No, it was surely about . . .

PAMELA: I can't wait. Tell me.

MURRAY: I don't understand you, Pamela. You seem to treat people as if they weren't there sometimes. As if they were just walk ons. What's happened?

PAMELA: Oh, Murray, do stop.

MURRAY: All these gibes, and immaturity—and your paternalist female ripeness.

PAMELA: Oh, very good, Murray. You sound like the character in your play.

MURRAY: You haven't even read it.

PAMELA: Yes I have. I read very slowly. Like everything else.

MURRAY: You can't be serious about Ladies' Services?

PAMELA: My dear, it's like going to the crimpers. Only more expensive. I may have to borrow some money from you.

MURRAY: I'll give it to you, of course.

PAMELA: You'll lend it to me. No, you won't. I'll borrow it from Bernard. I owe him enough already, but never mind.

MURRAY: You must.

PAMELA: I mustn't anything. I'd go to Wee Willie Wonder—

MURRAY: Wee who?

PAMELA: Wee Willie Wonder. My gynaecologist. But he'd only give me a lecture. Oh, he'd do it.

MURRAY: Is he a moralist too?

PAMELA: Not he. He's not one of those bear down and be joyful queens. He'd just lecture me.

MURRAY: What about?

PAMELA: Like you, like Mama and Constance. Except that he knows me better. Anyway, he's a nice sensitive man. He'll worry about me and reproach himself and I'll have him coming round to the house.

MURRAY: How did it happen?

PAMELA: What? Oh, guess.

MURRAY: Has it . . . ?

PAMELA: No, it's never happened before. At least I've not dried
up like an old prune after all. You've proved that. That
should please you. Still, even Wee Willie nods sometimes.
And it's a mysterious, capricious place in there. Especially
mine. Not surprising. It feels like a Bosch triptych often
enough. It's been better lately, I thought it was odd.

MURRAY: What do you mean: that should please you?

PAMELA: Oh, your eyes. Not just now. I used to see it in my
previous gentleman's face sometimes—before he left me.
When he was making love to me. He never said anything.
He was too reticent. I suppose it's a question of if you
become literally substantial they can luxuriate in their
abstraction with a nice trailing guide line to mother earth.
Trailing guide line, I've said that out of your play. There,
you see, I read very carefully. Do go, Murray. I want to get
undressed and I feel shy with you about the place and
Constance will be back and it's quite clear you're longing
to tell her. Well, I can't stop you. But I don't want her
solicitude and being practical and sustaining all of us. I'm
quite practical enough for myself. And I don't want to
sustain all of us. Even if you two do, and I know you will.
You're all bent on incest or some cosy hysteria. She's
bound to blub. You're not above it, and we'll all end up on
the floor embracing and comforting and rationalizing and
rumpled and snorting and jammed together and performing
autopsies and quite disgusting all of it. You both are.
Don't indulge her. Just because she demands it.

MURRAY: What?

PAMELA: She was brought up on the principle of fulfilment in as
many spheres as possible. As a statutory obligation. I'm
only saying don't always give in to her, and not now.
There isn't any statutory level of fulfilment we're entitled
to. I've tried to explain it to Constance. I've told her it
leads to excess and deception. It's difficult to talk to her

about a lot of things. She either reduces them to worthy
sounding principles or theorises them so that they relate
to any old thing. She's a very coarse woman, I'm afraid.

MURRAY: Have you ever told her?

PAMELA: No. It would hurt her. She'd mind. Besides, I'm fond
of her. I used to think we were alike. I take so long to find
things out. Dear God, I am always so far behind. She's
also rather coarse when she talks about sex. Oh, I know
what you think. Lust is o.k. by me. But not when it's
ambitious and gluttonous and avaricious. Then it's vulgar.
Very vulgar indeed. You shouldn't wear those shirts she
gives you. If you want to look really sharp, and you
obviously do, you need something a bit more expensive
than that. Give me your measurements. I'll go to Jermyn
Street in the morning. It'll give me something to do.

MURRAY: Pamela . . .

PAMELA: I haven't cleaned my teeth. Something in silk. A very
pale brown I think. And a dark, velvety tie. It would look
terribly good. You've not been around long enough. I
usually refit most of my gentlemen completely. Pity. Your
wardrobe needs a bit of a cast out. Don't let Constance
buy too many things for you. And simply remember, you
should know by now, you're twenty-nine, you're only a
few years older than me: one and one don't make two or
three. They sometimes don't even add up to one.
(*Phone rings.*)
Answer that, there's a good boy. If it's my Mother, I've
had an enormous bowl of nourishing soup, a boiled egg
and gone to bed to sleep it off.

MURRAY (*on phone*): Yes? Your agent . . .

PAMELA: Darling . . . That's good . . . Please . . . You're quite
wrong . . . No, don't come round . . . Listen, could you
hang on a minute . . . Murray, are you going?

MURRAY: I suppose I'd better.

PAMELA: You didn't mean that about coming round to my
house?

MURRAY: I don't know. Perhaps not, after all.

PAMELA: I wouldn't put it past Constance. Oh, and there's

Edith. Cheer up. We'll go out together sometimes. Not the
three of us. My nice coloured gentleman will be back soon.
You'll like him. He's frightfully New Statesman. Nice
though. Fastidious.

MURRAY: 'Bye, Pamela

PAMELA: 'Bye. (*On phone.*) No, Bernard, it's someone here.
Murray . . . Yes, that one. Some of my friends have got
real brains, they're not all sex-happy queens like you.
Though he's very sexy . . . No, nothing for you, darling. At
least, I don't fancy so . . . Actually, I've just read the play
he's written. I think you ought to look at it. I know you're
not but you might have some ideas. You know everybody.
And if you do do anything for him, I want a percentage . . .
I'm very poor, Bernard . . . What do you mean, I always
. . . He's just going . . . I'll give you his number . . . It'll be
worth your while. He's going to be very big. I know it.
You know what a success nose I have with people. Didn't
I tell you Abigail was going to be the biggest star since
Garbo . . . ? I know I told you not to take her on . . . I'd
have left you if you had . . . You're not that tasteless. Or
greedy. (*To* MURRAY.) What's your number, darling?
(*He looks at her and goes out.*)
(*to* BERNARD *on phone.*) Oh, I think he's gone. I'll give it to
you, the play. Look, darling, could you really help me? . . .
Could I come and stay with you for a few days? . . . I told
you, I'm fine. I just don't want to stay here any longer and
I can't face that little house for a bit. My Mama'll only
come round and she doesn't know you . . . Well, that's
your fortune . . . are you sure, really? . . . I won't stay
long and I'll not interfere with your love life, well I know
that's impossible . . . Who is he? . . . He sounds divine . . .
bless you . . . yes, I've got a paper and pencil. Right,
Ladies Services . . . Dr. Gradski . . .
(CONSTANCE *comes in carrying parcels,*)

CONSTANCE: Just missed Murray getting into a taxi.
(PAMELA *blows her a kiss.*)
Oh, sorry.
(*She goes into the kitchen, unwraps parcels of food, coming*

67

in and out.

PAMELA (*on phone*): Yes . . . who do I mention . . how much . . .
Dr. who? . . . You're kidding . . . yes . . . Don't seem
many Smiths or Browns . . . Sure these aren't the names of
agents you're giving me? . . . Oh, I know him, I met him
with you, the one who procures for you . . . oh come off
it . . . Yes . . . another . . . That'll do. I'll try these first . . .
and then I'll . . . might as well shop around. No . . .
Darling, don't, please. I'll make my own way. There's not
much to talk . . Oh, all right . . . half an hour . . . (*To*
CONSTANCE.) How are you?

CONSTANCE: I'm fine.

PAMELA: What's all that?

CONSTANCE: Goodies. I've just been to Fortnums. We're all
going to have a smashing meal. I bought some Dom
Perignon. I've just put it in the fridge. That isn't the one
you don't like, is it?

PAMELA: That's fine.

CONSTANCE: I'll ring Murray. I've been thinking about you all
day. I rushed away from my meeting. There's some scent
for you.

PAMELA: Darling—

CONSTANCE: I'm going to look after you. I've been talking to
Murray. He's very worried about you. I've been too soft
with you. I wished you'd been there this morning. I think
you'd have changed your mind.

PAMELA: I don't need looking after, darling. Lovely scent. I'll
put some on.

CONSTANCE: We owe it to one another.

PAMELA: No, we don't. You and Murray should have this place
to yourselves.

CONSTANCE: Nonsense. What could be nicer? Besides, Murray's
not getting rid of his flat. We both agreed on that.

PAMELA: I must go.

CONSTANCE: He doesn't want it.

PAMELA: Maybe not. I've got a few things packed.

CONSTANCE: But you don't mean you're going tonight? What
about dinner?

PAMELA: I'm sorry, but I've got to have dinner with Bernard. He wants me to meet some film producer. It's rather important. I'll have some of the Dom Perignon with a bit of ice in it though. That's sacrilege for you.

CONSTANCE: Pamela, what's wrong? My darling. Tell me. Why don't you talk to me?

PAMELA: I've stayed long enough.

CONSTANCE: What is it? I thought you were happy with me. We do get on, don't we?

PAMELA: Sure. But I need to get away for a bit.

CONSTANCE: You mean a holiday? We could all go together, Why don't we? What a super idea.

PAMELA: I'm going with Bernard to the South of France. One of his friends has got a villa. I don't think it's what Pauline calls your scene. It's not really mine.

CONSTANCE: Murray would be fascinated I'm sure.

PAMELA: I think Murray might inhibit them a bit. No, I'll just sit by the pool and become a golden girl again. I've been looking at my body . . . look at it. A sort of dirty yellow cigarette stain colour.

CONSTANCE: You look stunning.

PAMELA: Sorry about your dinner. You and Murray can have a nice candlelight session alone together. You don't mind Bernard coming round?

CONSTANCE: No. I'm a bit dazed. I don't know whether I want to cook now.

PAMELA: You must feed up Murray. Spoil him. He likes spoiling. And why not?

CONSTANCE: I'll pack for you, if you must . . .

PAMELA: Don't bother. I'll leave most of it . . . for now. Just talk to me while I undress.

She moves between her bedroom and the drawing room dressing and packing in a casual way, talking. At one point, in the bedroom she is naked. CONSTANCE *wanders about following her, rather helplessly, smoking and watching her every movement.*

CONSTANCE: I brought you the evening papers.

PAMELA: More rave notices for Lady Tinker-Bell, I suppose?

CONSTANCE: Oh, yes, "all that's permanently in the air".

PAMELA: Did you and Murray enjoy it?

CONSTANCE: I think Murray quite liked it. He liked her, anyway, you'll be sorry to hear.

PAMELA: I'm not sorry.

CONSTANCE: I think he thought she'd be good in his play. I think I see what you mean. But she certainly gets the audience and the critics.

PAMELA: You bet. Went out of their frigid little minds. Still, I suppose there's always hope on Sunday.

CONSTANCE: I see you've got all the papers then.

PAMELA: Yes, Mama brought them. She seemed to think I'd want to see them. She's also a great fan of Abigail's too. Natch. Bet she wishes she had a daughter like that.

CONSTANCE: This one says something good about the play too . . . "Finely wrought and blessedly well constructed".

PAMELA: That means it's like a travelling clock. You can see all the works. That way you know it must keep the right time. (*She goes into the bedroom.* CONSTANCE *watches her from the doorway with the papers.*)

CONSTANCE: . . . "What a relief to hear every syllable superbly and uniquely delivered."

PAMELA: Why doesn't he own up he's deaf? He was the only critic who couldn't hear Orme. And he had a voice like a ton of Welsh nuts. I don't mind people being old as long as they're not bullying with it.

CONSTANCE: I think there's actually one with "mystery behind the eyes". Yes, here it is: "a fugitive, self-scrutinizing mystery".

PAMELA: Self-absorbed he means. He's hardly taken his eyes off the leading man all evening. He's the one who made that little play I was in sound so worthy and full of painful silences and hauntingly expressed, delicate agonies or something. Kept them away in droves. Mind you, it *was* a bit worthy, all greys and browns and sort of obsessed with being rarefied and staring you out with austerity. I got good notices, specially from him. I knew I would. It was a sympathetic, bearing down part. All I had to do was

70

upstage myself and keep a straight back. Sounds like cricket doesn't it. I got stuff about my repose and troubled enchantment and the impression of a powerful intelligence in perfect unison with heartaching turmoil. Something like that.

CONSTANCE: Well, you remembered it.

PAMELA: Even I remember some jokes. Actually, I wasn't really thinking about anything. I just kept trying to think what Orme would have done. He didn't think too much of it. He said you're giving your critics' performance. So, I said I know, but I've got to get on sometimes. And he didn't say anything. Except: that's all right. As long as you know it. Try and give the audience the real thing sometimes. Would you like me to do Abigail for you?

(CONSTANCE *laughs*.)

You can't miss if you do that. They go off their heads.

CONSTANCE: Gosh, you've got a beautiful body.

PAMELA: As I say, you have to be frigid to be one of them.

CONSTANCE: You really are permanently brown all over. You haven't got those awful bra cup marks.

PAMELA: You need to be three things: timid, agressive and frigid. T.A.F. Like Welsh.

CONSTANCE: This one seems to have lost the point completely.

PAMELA: Probably wasn't listening, poor darling. Who is it? Oh, he's the one who sends me those dreadful telly plays he writes. Takes the part for the whole—as the actress said to the critic. Don't look so glum. I've just made a joke. I thought you were mad about jokes?

CONSTANCE: I hate to see you go. Do these upset you?

PAMELA: It takes more than an Abigail to make me give up. It's all like the weather. As for them, there's something fundamentally wrong with you if you want to do that. Something missing. I've noticed it. When you meet them. Impotence. That's why when they've been really nasty, they try to ingratiate if you're ever unlucky enough to meet one. "Oh, did I say that? I'm sure I've said other things. I've always admired your work".

CONSTANCE: You're looking better.

PAMELA: I feel it. Thinking of Abigail and all those people being hoaxed. Put some ice in that lovely Dom Perignon.

CONSTANCE: Good idea. You seem almost superstitious about her.

PAMELA: How?

CONSTANCE: Well, it's as if she didn't take everybody in, you'd be disappointed.

PAMELA: I suppose I would; they might have taste.

CONSTANCE: Wouldn't it be better if they did?

PAMELA: It would. But they haven't.

CONSTANCE: It seems to give you back your energy. You're so afraid of losing it.

PAMELA: So would you. It's a delicate plant. Not like your great climbing tree.

CONSTANCE: No. I have to flog mine. You're right. But good fortune, if you like, seems to fill you with dread.

PAMELA: Dread never is very far away, is it? Here's to success! Um. Delicious.

CONSTANCE: It'll seem strange not having you drink champagne about the place. We usually drink whisky when we're together. Murray, I mean. It's only when we're with you. Perhaps you've converted us. He really loves you.

PAMELA: You can't afford it. Champagne I mean. Well, not Dom Perignon.

CONSTANCE: Darling, please stay. You need love more than anyone I've ever known. And looking after. We'll both do it.

PAMELA: You look after Murray. He's the sort who needs it. Clever men need a lot of pampering. They have a hard time in some ways, I think.

CONSTANCE: Pamela, why don't you play the part in his play?

PAMELA: I thought he liked the idea of Abigail? If he can get her.

CONSTANCE: I think you'd be much better.

PAMELA: Tell a management that.

CONSTANCE: Gosh, actresses get ready quickly.

PAMELA: We have to.

CONSTANCE: You did like it, didn't you?

72

PAMELA: Yes. I'm giving it to Bernard. He might have some ideas.

CONSTANCE: What did you think of it?

PAMELA: Actually, he did ask me if I'd do it.

CONSTANCE: Well?

PAMELA: I don't really understand it, Constance. Perhaps I'm not clever enough.

CONSTANCE: You don't mean it. You don't like it. Did you tell him?

PAMELA: No. Why? What's my opinion! You like it. I'm sure a lot of people will.

CONSTANCE: But why? He respects your opinion.

PAMELA: Well, tell him not to.

CONSTANCE: What's wrong with it?

PAMELA: Oh, please. Don't hedge me in. Authors should never go peddling in the market place.

CONSTANCE: I know. It's vulgar.

PAMELA: Quite. Oh, all right, if you must. I think it's, yes, clever. It's full of erudite banalities. It's not a play, it's a posture by a clever annotator, a labeller. People sit around and make up Freudian epigrams about one another. It's written by someone thinking about writing it instead of thinking about whatever it's about. Do I make myself incomprehensible? I'm afraid it's catching from that script. I'm sorry, darling.

CONSTANCE: It seems as if just everything is over. You're going away. The recess'll be over soon.

PAMELA: It was never to be a permanent arrangement.

CONSTANCE: No. Perhaps I had deluded myself that it would be somehow.

PAMELA: It's always tempting but one must guard against the more likely possibilities.

CONSTANCE: Pamela, why were you taking down those phone numbers?

PAMELA: Oh, my God. I must ring them before I go. Ladies' Services, darling. Somebody in need.

CONSTANCE: Who?

PAMELA: No one you know.

CONSTANCE: Who?

PAMELA: Audrey—the girl in the crimpers. Silly girl. I thought they all took the pill those girls now.

CONSTANCE: Aren't you taking a risk.

PAMELA: Darling, I'm just helping the poor girl out. Hope she can afford it. Oh, don't look like that. What does one do— wait for the third reading in the Lords?

CONSTANCE: Darling, you will keep in touch, won't you?

PAMELA: Of course. I always do. Don't blub, darling. Have a nice dinner and a cuddle with Murray.

CONSTANCE: Sorry. I blub too easily.

PAMELA: Yes. You do. You must learn to do it without letting your mascara run. It's quite an easy trick. I'll show you. (*Doorbell rings.*)

CONSTANCE: Damn! Don't go yet. Please. When's Bernard coming?

PAMELA: I said half an hour. He'll be late.

CONSTANCE: Might be Murray. Hope so. I'll make *him* talk you out of it.

She goes to the door. EDWARD *stands there, slightly drunk with* ABIGAIL *beside him. She is dressed in Men's Carnaby Street clothes. She also wears a theatrical moustache.*

It is almost possible to mistake her for a man at first glance, but only just. It is just the starlit ABIGAIL.)

EDWARD: Hi.

CONSTANCE: Edward. Come in. What——?

EDWARD: Is Pamela up?

CONSTANCE: She's just dressing. I don't know . . . Is it . . . Why Abigail!

ABIGAIL: Constance, love!

CONSTANCE: Do you know, I really didn't recognise you. Good heavens. You look, you look marvellous. What, what happened?

EDWARD: She looks a gas doesn't she? Pamela! Don't say anything—(*To* CONSTANCE.)

(*They come in.*)

How are you, darling? Better?

PAMELA: Hello, Eddie. I'm all right darling. Just coming.

Constance, give him some of your expensive champagne.

CONSTANCE: I'll get it.

(PAMELA *appears. She stares at* ABIGAIL, *who is seated in the centre of the room.*)

PAMELA: Who's your friend? Good God! . . .

CONSTANCE: I was wondering if you'd be taken in. I was. Just for a moment. Doesn't she look marvellous.

EDWARD: We thought it was fun.

PAMELA: Hilarious. Where have you been like that?

ABIGAIL: Well, darling, how are you, you look really beautiful, honestly more than ever. I adore your hair.

PAMELA: I haven't been to the crimpers for two weeks.

ABIGAIL: Well, we had this night last night, you see, what with everything.

CONSTANCE: Oh, congratulations.

PAMELA: Yes.

ABIGAIL: Thank you, my darlings.

PAMELA: Did you get my telegram?

ABIGAIL: Yes, darling. Bless you. Isn't it marvellous? I can't believe it.

PAMELA: I don't know why. I find it only too believable. I thought I'd forgotten to send that telegram.

ABIGAIL: Eddie's been super. We had an absolute rave night. The management gave a party. That looked like being a bit draggy.

EDWARD: I'll say.

ABIGAIL: No, but darling, everyone was so sweet. And, you know, all the old excitement, and, oh well, you know what it's like, Pamela.

EDWARD: Hey, Connie, where's your record player. We just bought a fabulous record.

ABIGAIL: Oh, yes, Eddie. Do play it for them. Pamela will adore it. I'm mad about it.

PAMELA: So you did what?

ABIGAIL: Oh, yes, well there was the first night, and, well it was extraordinary. I don't remember much. I know I cried at the call.

EDWARD: They were hanging from the ceiling. It was a cert.

75

You could tell.

ABIGAIL: You know that feeling?

PAMELA: Yes.

ABIGAIL: Well, I couldn't get out of my dressing room for hours. Then we finally got to this party. They were getting a bit narked I think, but it was lovely when we got there. Oh, everyone was so happy. Somehow, good things, well they simply change everyone, don't they? I mean they do. Everyone was just pleased and happy and I didn't care what happened. Then we left finally. Eddie drove us down to get the papers. Though everyone said we needn't bother. And, of course, it was super. We all went back, well, some of us, to Eddie's and we just went dotty all night. Eddie and I didn't go to bed at all.

CONSTANCE: How do you feel?

ABIGAIL: Wonderful! Oh, I do think people are really *it*. Absolutely. I do! Oh, champagne, how delicious. So, yes we had champagne and Eddie cooked bacon and eggs with it for breakfast. And he said let's go out and buy anything we want. We're loaded. We can have anything we want. And, oh, so we did. We bought pictures and rugs and I bought a lovely ring and Eddie bought a fabulous cigarette lighter. Oh, we went to galleries and I bought some clothes. Then Eddie said we must have lunch at the Caprice. We hadn't booked a table and it was packed but we just walked in. We saw loads of people, didn't we, Eddie?

EDWARD: Yeh.

ABIGAIL: Then we saw a bit of some Swedish movie. It had some thrilling things with a girl having a baby.

PAMELA: Really?

ABIGAIL: I thought it was rather beautiful. But Eddie got bored and fell asleep and I woke him up, and we bought these super records. And, oh, yes this, well, we thought it would be fun if I changed. You know, there's a picture of me in every paper today. So we dropped in at Wig Creations for the moustache, then got a taxi to Carnaby Street. Walked all the way to Charing Cross Road. Not a head turned.

76

Isn't it marvellous?

PAMELA: Fantastic.

ABIGAIL: That's right, Eddie. Oh, it's marvellous, Listen to this, Pamela. You'll go dotty. Constance . . . Eddie.

(EDDIE *and* ABIGAIL *dance to the record.* CONSTANCE *and* PAMELA *watch.*)

EDWARD (*presently*): How are you, Pamela.

ABIGAIL: Isn't it divine? Yes, are you all right, darling?

PAMELA: Sure.

ABIGAIL: Oh, my God!

EDWARD: What is it?

ABIGAIL: Oh my God. Pamela! What have I done?

PAMELA: Tell me.

ABIGAIL: I should have gone to your father's Memorial!

PAMELA: I shouldn't worry. You had a better time.

ABIGAIL: But I should have gone.

PAMELA: Why? He didn't want anyone to go. I'm sure he would have approved of your day, Abigail.

ABIGAIL: But don't you understand. I was supposed to read one of the lessons.

CONSTANCE: Abigail—

PAMELA: I'm sure there were too many.

ABIGAIL: How *awful*. Pamela, what can I say?

PAMELA: Don't.

ABIGAIL: But I was asked.

PAMELA: They must have managed. No one mentioned it to me.

ABIGAIL: Darling. Eddie, turn that off. He really was the most marvellous actor. My Father was mad about him. I scarcely saw him.

PAMELA: No.

ABIGAIL: And are you all right, darling?

PAMELA: Fine.

CONSTANCE: She's a bit done in.

ABIGAIL: Eddie. Darlings, I must go. Look at the time. I've got a performance. Can we get a taxi here?

CONSTANCE: You'll get one in the street.

PAMELA: I should take your moustache off.

ABIGAIL: Darling. Bless you.

(*Embraces all round.*)

Sorry we barged in. Just wanted to see if you were all right.

EDWARD: My idea really.

PAMELA: I know. Thanks, Edward.

ABIGAIL: 'Bye, darling.

(*She and* EDWARD *do a musical exit. Then he comes back for the record.*)

(*Pause.*)

CONSTANCE: I think they've finished off the champagne.

PAMELA: I've got a last bottle. At the back at the bottom.

CONSTANCE: I'll get it. Can't you put Bernard off? I'll ring Murray.

PAMELA: I'm all ready.

CONSTANCE: Don't let Abigail break everything up.

PAMELA: I don't think she has.

CONSTANCE: Don't be hurt by it.

PAMELA: My dear girl, I promise you I'm not. Bernard's bound to be late.

CONSTANCE: There: here's to us.

PAMELA: To us all.

CONSTANCE: Are you taking the books with you? Orme's?

PAMELA: Oh, they'll go in Bernard's car. In the back somewhere.

CONSTANCE: Why do you suppose he goes around with Abigail?

PAMELA: Why do you think? Why does Murray want her for his play? At least she's alive in her way. Even he gets bored with his dollies. The thing about them is they really are mostly wooden. Abigail isn't wooden.

CONSTANCE: Please ring him up. Stay tonight.

PAMELA: It's too late. He'll be on his way. Look at that: Portia's solicitude for Brutus.

CONSTANCE: It looks a bit more than solicitude.

PAMELA: Oh, Orme couldn't bear her. He said her underwear was never clean. I can quite believe it.

CONSTANCE: What does he say about Abigail.

PAMELA: We don't talk about it. We didn't talk about it. Kingsway Theatre. Founded on the French of Gabriel Vardie. Queens Theatre. Meggie Albenesi. He knew all all about her. Remembrance. That sounds good. Oh, he's

78

playing a wog here. Count Stefano Ciffoni. He liked that. There he is on the West coast of Scotland. That's his place. His bleeding piece of earth, he called it. Well, *he* thought it was funny.

CONSTANCE: What were his big roles, really?

PAMELA: He was big in all of them. Even when he was bad. Oh, I suppose you mean, well, Shylock, Macbeth of course, Brutus oh yes, Hotspur and a very funny Malvolio.

CONSTANCE: What was *that* called?

PAMELA: "The Real Thing". Aah, here we are. The Countess lights upon—lights upon already—the Count in a compromising situation. Oh, Orme. She looks het up all right. Drunk I expect. Yes, look, see he's having to hold her up. He always did. Yes, it's the last act. What's new in the next session?

CONSTANCE: Oh, pretty heavy.

PAMELA: You won't have much time then?

CONSTANCE: No, what about your film?

PAMELA: Don't know yet. I expect I'll do a telly. Here we are: "The Real Thing." "Think, Ella, there *is* no inheritance, nothing, only my debts and no career. Just the poor son of a parson, an ex-captain. Now that Jock Crawley has deprived me of my one chance, my one hope of happiness and redeeming myself, there is nothing left for me to do. Only go out of your life. No, I want you. I want you to be my wife. That is not possible. I *want* your life. Ella, Oh Ella, you are a magnificent woman. A gem." *She* had mystery behind the eyes even then. "And so are you David. All that a woman could ever want. A real gem. Not paste. But the real thing, Davie. The real thing."

CONSTANCE: Perhaps it should have been called "A Real Gem".

PAMELA: No. "The Real Thing" was better. Oh, here's one of his great flops. His own adaptation of "The Brothers Karamazov." Lost all his savings in that. Here we are, here's the critics: "A gloomy piece, which will only, we confidently predict, achieve a limited hold on the public." It certainly did. Lost all his savings. His own management, you see. And his own wife dunning him for money all the

79

time. He was always having affairs with actresses.

CONSTANCE: Oh, Pamela . . what are we all going to do?

PAMELA: You'll go back after the recess. That's what you'll do. It's getting better all the time.

CONSTANCE: Is it? I don't know.

PAMELA: Anyway, someone said, I think: "The worst has already happened". Or something. He adored actresses. But he didn't like the idea of marrying them. At least, I think he did, but he didn't meet her. That was the trouble with Mama. Just because she was always on about Kokoschka and Thomas Mann and the texture of life in a Socialist society, he was taken in by it. He thought she was not only cleverer than his other ladies, but cleverer than him.

CONSTANCE: What's she really like?

PAMELA: Daft as a brush. The old man had more in the way he held a tennis racket than every letter she ever wrote to the papers. From unemployment in the Highlands to bed wetting. Thank God for Orme, I was born before Dr. Spock. He was through that. Please don't cry, dear. Or I'll have to go before Bernard turns up.

CONSTANCE: It all seems so wrong.

(*Bell rings.*)

PAMELA: I'll go.

(*She goes.* CONSTANCE *can't move. The door reveals* BERNARD.)

Darling, you're on time.

BERNARD: Darling—for you, anything. What are you up to, you naughty girl? I'm going to give you a tough evening.

PAMELA: Oh no, you're not. You can just tell me the news and then I'm going to bed early. You'll have things to do anyway. You know Constance.

BERNARD: Hello. Where do you want to eat? Is that all the stuff you've got?

PAMELA: I'm sending back for the rest. How about the Armpit Restaurant?

BERNARD: My dear, I've got so much to *tell* you. How about Abigail Ratatouilles?

80

PAMELA: Don't tell me.

BERNARD: Shall I take these?

PAMELA: Darling, would you? I'll get my fur coats. Always need *them*. It gets cold, even in the South of France.

CONSTANCE: Won't you have a drink before you go?

PAMELA: Bernard doesn't drink, isn't it dreary? He's so obsessed with his figure, which isn't so hot anyway. And also his performance. About which who knows.

BERNARD: You might find out one day, darling. Don't think I can't. You're looking fabulous. Doesn't she?

CONSTANCE: She does. Pamela?

PAMELA: Could you take these, Bernard? I'll just say goodbye to Constance.

BERNARD: Right, I'll be downstairs. 'Night, Constance.

CONSTANCE: Goodnight, Bernard.

(*He goes.*)

Oh, my dear. It isn't right.

PAMELA: Sh. There. I'll teach you that trick the next time. Take care.

CONSTANCE: Take care.

(*They embrace.*)

PAMELA: Oh, Bernard will look after me.

(*She goes out.* CONSTANCE *drinks the rest of her champagne. She goes to the telephone and dials.*)

CONSTANCE (*on phone*): Darling? You're there . . . No, I'm o.k. . . . I arranged a dinner for Pamela and she's gone . . . Yes, left . . . I don't know . . . How do I know . . . I don't know what she's bent on or anything . . come on over . . . yes, now, please . . . I love you . . . I ache for you . . . Do you? Thank heaven for that . . . Darling . . . oh, my darling . . . Pamela's going to give me a lesson . . . yes, right . . . Don't be long . . .

CURTAIN.

THE HOTEL IN AMSTERDAM
A Play

CAST

HOTEL PORTER
LAURIE
MARGARET
ANNIE
GUS
AMY
DAN
GILLIAN
WAITER

ACT ONE

The drawing-room of a suite in a large, first-class hotel in Amster-dam. It is a fairly cheerful room as such hotel rooms go with bright prints, plenty of low lamps and furnished in a rather friendly com-bination of thirtyish and tactful Hotel Empire. Three separate bedrooms lead off. The door to the hotel corridor opens and a PORTER *enters with a trolley filled with luggage. He is followed rather tentatively by three couples,* LAURIE *and* MARGARET; GUS *and* ANNIE; *and* DAN *and* AMY. *They are all fairly attractively dressed and near or around forty but none middle-aged. In fact, they are pretty flash and vigorous looking. Perhaps* GUS *and* MARGARET *less so than the others. This is partly because he is dressed a bit more conservatively than the other two men and she is visibly pregnant, though not unattractive. The* PORTER *looks for instructions about the baggage. He looks for the leader and decides on* GUS.

PORTER: Sir?

GUS: I'm sorry?

LAURIE: I think it's the baggage, Gus.

GUS: Oh.

MARGARET: Well, tell him darling.

GUS: No, it's all right. Now, let's see.

ANNIE: Well, don't let's make an operation out of it. Those are ours. There, porter. Those two.

GUS: Yes, ah but where are we all going to go? We don't, I mean we haven't had a look yet.

LAURIE: Why don't we sort them out and decide afterwards?

MARGARET: Brilliant.

ANNIE: Some men are brilliant, aren't they?

AMY: Can I help?

MARGARET: No. Gus can manage.

GUS: Yes. Well it's just a question of sorting out the rooms isn't it? They're all there.

ANNIE: I should hope so. We're paying enough for them.

MARGARET: Well, don't let him stand there, darling.

GUS: Well, we think we'll have a look at the rooms first and then decide where we're all going and—

ANNIE: That'll take hours with Gus.

MARGARET: No. It won't. Look, porter, just put them all down on the floor and we'll sort them out ourselves.

PORTER: Yes, madam.

GUS: Oh, do you think we should?

LAURIE: Yes, much quicker.

GUS: We'll have to carry it.

LAURIE: That's true. I want a drink really. Have you got any—

GUS: What—a drink? No, but we can order some now.

LAURIE: No. You know. Change. Tip.

GUS: Oh, no, no I haven't. Let's see. No, I used it on the taxi.

LAURIE: Darling?

MARGARET: You know I haven't.

ANNIE: I might have. Did you forget, Laurie?

MARGARET: Of course he didn't. He just didn't like to ask.

ANNIE: Why on earth not?

MARGARET: He's terrified no one's going to speak English.

ANNIE: You don't think they're going to speak Dutch, do you?

LAURIE: I suppose not. She's quite right though. I just feel I ought to and then I dry up. France is worst because it really seems so thick not to.

DAN: Like Americans.

LAURIE: Exactly. And they're so foul, the French I mean. If you do have a bit of a go, they despise you and pretend they they don't know. A waiter in Paris actually corrected me saying Vodka once. After all, that's a Russian word.

ANNIE: I shouldn't let it worry you.

LAURIE: Well, it does.

ANNIE: Gus is very good. Bit slow but you're full of initiative always aren't you, darling?

GUS: Yes, I don't think I have that trouble so much. You can usually get someone to understand—especially nowadays.

LAURIE: That's the trouble. Amy, what should we give?

GUS: I looked up the exchange.

AMY: Here.

(*She tips the* PORTER, *who looks neither pleased nor displeased.*)

ANNIE: Thank heavens. Now Laurie can breathe and we can look around.

LAURIE: Just a minute. Do we all want a drink?

MARGARET: You mean: you do.

GUS: I don't know. Do we, darling?

ANNIE: You bet. After that journey. Aeroplanes!

GUS: Margaret?

MARGARET: No. I'm not.

GUS: Of course. Would you like something else?

MARGARET: Just mineral water. Perrier. Something.

GUS: Amy?

LAURIE: I know Amy will and Dan's tongue's dropping out.

MARGARET: You hope.

LAURIE: I can see it from here. Why don't we—

MARGARET: No. It's too expensive.

LAURIE: But we ought to celebrate getting here. After all, we're all in one piece, we're all together, we've escaped and—

ANNIE: Nobody knows we're here.

LAURIE: No one. Absolutely no one.

MARGARET: Well, that's not true.

LAURIE (*to* PORTER): Don't go. Well, no one who matters or will let on. Amy saw to that, didn't you?

ANNIE: Oh, come on let's order. I'll have a whisky sour.

LAURIE: Oh, isn't that going to be difficult?

ANNIE: Difficult? A whisky sour?

LAURIE: If we all have something different—

GUS: I see what he means.

DAN: Yes. Reinforcements.

LAURIE: Perhaps we could vote on it. All the same thing.

ANNIE: I *have* voted. I'm not being democratic just for convenience.

LAURIE: What about the rest. Amy?

AMY: I really don't mind.

LAURIE: Good girl. And Dan, you'll drink anything. Right? Scotch?

DAN: O.K.

LAURIE: Right, then so will I. Gus?

GUS: All right. But don't forget Margaret's Perrier.

LAURIE: Shall I?

ANNIE: We would like one whisky sour, one Perrier water, a
bottle of J. & B. or Cutty Sark. Some ice and some soda.
To LAURIE.) Happy?

LAURIE: Make it two bottles, we'll need them.

ANNIE: Two bottles.

LAURIE: And quickly please, if you can.

PORTER: Yes, sir.

GUS: Well now.

ANNIE: Let's look at the room. All right, Margaret?

MARGARET: Fine. Right.

ANNIE: You have first pick.

GUS: Oh, yes.

ANNIE: I don't mind. As long as the bed's big and comfortable.

LAURIE: I do.

MARGARET: You would; spoiled.

LAURIE: Well, let's get it over.

MARGARET: Don't fret, darling. Your drink will be here soon.

LAURIE: God, I hate travelling.

MARGARET: Well, you've arrived. Relax.

LAURIE: Yes, that's true isn't it? I suppose we really have. What
a relief. All those passports and tickets and airport buses
and being bossed about. Air hostesses—I'd love to rape an
air hostess.

GUS: Really? I don't mean about air hostesses. I rather enjoy
all that travel guff.

DAN: You would. Public school.

MARGARET: Now then, Dan, don't be chippy. You're very lucky
to be with your betters.

DAN: I know it. I hate the working classes. That's why I got
out.

AMY: You can never get out.

DAN: I did. They're an unlovable, whining, blackmailing shower.

ANNIE: What's he talking about?

MARGARET: Just being chippy.

LAURIE: Don't keep saying that. You should see *my* horrible family.

MARGARET: I have and now you're both being chippy.

LAURIE: We're both just saying we've got horrible families and that you're lucky to have nice, gentle, civilized, moderate parents like yours. Right, Dan?

DAN: Right.

MARGARET: Oh, my goodness, class solidarity. Anyway, my mother's not that hot.

LAURIE: She's divine.

MARGARET: Well, you think so. She's just dull and sporty.

LAURIE: She's not. She's extremely attractive and intelligent.

DAN: Not like my mum—scheming old turd.

LAURIE: And your mum's so ugly.

DAN: Telling me.

LAURIE: Funny really because you're not.

ANNIE: He's beautiful.

LAURIE: Mine's got a very mean little face. Celebrates every effect, plays up all the time, to the gallery, do anything for anything. Self-involved, bullying.

MARGARET: Oh, come off it.

LAURIE: I suppose you think her face is pitted by the cares of working class life and bringing up her sons on National Assistance. Well, it isn't. She has that face there because there's a mean, grudging, grasping nature behind it.

MARGARET: I don't know why nice men don't like their mothers.

ANNIE: Gus likes his.

LAURIE: That's because she's probably nice.

ANNIE: She isn't bad.

GUS: No. I suppose she isn't really.

LAURIE: And he's a bit queer too, remember.

ANNIE: That's true.

MARGARET: But you always say you are a bit.

LAURIE: So I am. But not as much as Gus.

AMY: What about Dan?

LAURIE: Well—either less than Gus or me. Or much more. He's more elusive. I mean Gus is so obvious. Those clothes. That's real conservatism.

GUS: Are they awful?

91

MARGARET: You look dishy.

LAURIE: I think my mother *would* have put me off women for life. I mean just to think of swimming about inside that repulsive thing for nine months.

MARGARET: Please.

LAURIE: But I think when I was quite young I must have decided she was nothing to do with women at all. That's why the real thing was such an eternal surprise.

MARGARET: She'd love this. You usually butter her up.

LAURIE: She doesn't give a twopenny fart. Excuse me—I think I'm going to . . . It's the idea of my mother. Don't worry, I'll tell her before she dies. No. I die. She'll outlive me for years.

DAN: My mother would have made a good air hostess.

LAURIE: Your mother! Listen, my mother should have been Chief Stewardess on Monster's Airlines. She'd have kept you waiting in every bus, withheld information and liquor, snapped at you, and smirked at you meaninglessly or simply just ignored you.

DAN: Have you ever thought of airlines for homosexuals?

LAURIE: I say: what a splendid idea. You could call it El Fag Airlines.

ANNIE: Gus could be a stewardess.

LAURIE: We'd design him a divine outfit. I say I feel better already.

MARGARET: Don't get carried away. The holiday's only just started.

LAURIE: The great escape you mean.

GUS: You mean all the aircrew would be chaps?

DAN: *And* the passengers.

LAURIE: Why don't we start it? Fly El Fag. The Airlines that floats just for HIM!

GUS: It's not bad is it? I say, we're getting our wind back aren't we? Just starting to feel safe I suppose.

DAN: We're really here.

LAURIE: Really here.

ANNIE: I don't know who's more astonished that we've all scarpered. Us or whether *he* will be.

AMY: K.L. will be *pretty* astonished when he finds out.

MARGARET: Let's face it: so are we.

ANNIE: We do sound a bit amazed at our own naughtiness.

LAURIE: No, we're not.

MARGARET: Yes, we are. Come on. You are.

LAURIE: No, we are relieved, unburdened, we've managed to slough off that monster for a few days. We have escaped, we deserve it, after all this time. Just to be somewhere he doesn't know where any of us are. Can't get near us, call us, ring us, come round, write. Nothing. Nix. For a few blessed days. No K.L. in our lives.

MARGARET: You make it more cowardly than it is.

LAURIE: So what if it is?

ANNIE: No. It isn't. We all deserve to escape. After all, he *is* the biggest, most poisonous, voracious, Machiavellian dinosaur in movies. And we all know what that means.

LAURIE: Quite.

ANNIE: Sorry, Amy. I know he's your boss.

DAN: He seems to be everybody's boss.

AMY: Poor Dan.

ANNIE: Yes. Married to the boss's secretary. That's probably the worst position of all.

MARGARET: You and I are in the same position.

GUS: I suppose we all play different roles to the dinosaur. But they're still roles.

DAN: Amy adores him.

ANNIE: So does everybody. I do. And Margaret does. Gus can't live without him. And Laurie tries to pretend he can.

LAURIE: I can.

ANNIE: I wonder if you will.

LAURIE: I have before and it sure didn't kill me.

MARGARET: I don't think I could bear any more recriminations.

ANNIE: But the rest of us are still supposed to be friends.

GUS: It's difficult isn't it? Perhaps Laurie can come to some understanding.

LAURIE: Not this time, buddy, He's had it.

GUS: I don't know how we'll cope when we get back.

ANNIE: Darling. We've only just arrived.

93

MARGARET: How amused he'd be. Here we are congratulating ourselves on escaping from him and we've hardly stopped talking about him since we left Liverpool Street.

LAURIE: I wouldn't feel flattered to hear *what* we've said.

ANNIE: He'd be amused certainly.

LAURIE: Amy, you are sure?

AMY: Absolutely sure.

LAURIE: It would be great if he suddenly walked through that door while we were laughing and joking all together.

AMY: He won't.

GUS: What a thought.

MARGARET: Poor Amy. She's the real Judas amongst us. After all, she *is* his secretary. *We're* conspirators.

LAURIE: I don't see that she's been disloyal. So what if she has! That cock's crowed a bit too often for every one of us. *And* everyone else. Those he's victimized at one time or another. Oh, he'll find another spare eunuch knocking around London. The world's full of hustlers and victims all beavering away to be pressed into K.L.'s service. Someone always wants to be useful or flattered or gulled or just plain whipped slowly to death or cast out into the knackers yard by King Sham. Well, let him go ahead and get himself crucified this time. I know him not.

ANNIE: What do you mean?

LAURIE: What I say.

MARGARET: He won't.

GUS: Won't what?

LAURIE: Get himself crucified.

GUS: No, I suppose not.

ANNIE: No.

DAN: Pity.

AMY: He'll be all right. He'll find someone.

GUS: I say, do you know we haven't looked at the view yet. It's rather good.

MARGARET: So it is.

AMY: We're really here.

DAN: I wish you'd stop saying that. Of course we're here. You made all the superb arrangements didn't you?

MARGARET: Yes, thanks, Amy.

LAURIE: Hear, hear. Thank you, Amy.

ANNIE: Well, screw the view, we haven't looked at the rooms yet.

MARGARET: Yes, we must do that now.

ANNIE: Won't K.L. be furious when he can't get hold of you over the weekend? He knows you never go away.

AMY: I said I was staying with some relatives in Yorkshire.

ANNIE: But you're a hopeless liar. You're so transparent.

AMY: I hinted it was really a lover.

LAURIE: Oh, he'd like that. More demolition around the joint.

AMY: Yes, he was rather intrigued. So he didn't ask any questions.

MARGARET: Not even where to get hold of you?

AMY: I said there was no phone. But I'd ring him.

MARGARET: Then won't you have to?

AMY: Well, of course, he'll be furious when I don't. I'll have to say I wasn't well.

LAURIE: That won't wash. He'll ring Dan to stir it up.

AMY: I don't think he'd do that. He wouldn't want to mess things up if he really thinks I've got a lover and Dan doesn't know about it.

ANNIE: Don't fancy your first morning back, with your shorthand pad when your boss has been deprived and rejected of men all weekend and you not on the phone having a bit on the side and not even confiding in him. He'll be *very* hurt.

AMY: Oh, dear. Yes. He will.

LAURIE: So what. Say you had the curse and it ruined the entire rendezvous. That would appeal to him.

AMY: Wouldn't wash. He knows my calendar better than I do.

DAN: Knows your miserable little face, you mean.

MARGARET: Aren't they charming?

ANNIE: Did you know that air hostesses have holy travail with the curse?

LAURIE: Really? Good.

ANNIE: Seriously. To do with the air pressure or something.

LAURIE: Good. Jolly good!

ANNIE: Either don't get it for months on end and worry themselves to death in case they're up the spout . . .

LAURIE: Fancy a pregnant air hostess. Think how high and mighty she'd be. Putting her feet up and pecking at all the customers' canapés.

ANNIE: Or they get it twice a week.

DAN: Do you mind. I feel a pain coming on.

ANNIE: Wish you did. Then you wouldn't jeer at poor little Amy when she's boo-hooing all over K.L.'s office.

DAN: Thank God they don't have women pilots.

GUS: The Russians do.

LAURIE: Remember: never travel on Rusky Airlines. Keep to El Fag.

DAN: Or you might go up front and see a little bundle of Russian misery crying its eyes out over the controls.

LAURIE: All misted up and locking herself in the loo. Worse than seeing a little yellow face turn round and grin at you.

ANNIE: Like the Lost Horizon.

LAURIE: Our bloody drinks are lost. Where is that hopeless Hollander? Do you suppose he understood us?

MARGARET: Of course he understood us. This isn't Bournemouth.

(*Knock.* WAITER *enters.*)

GUS: Ah. There we are. Good evening.

WAITER: Good evening, sir.

MARGARET: Now you can relax.

GUS: I say this is Haig. Didn't you order—

LAURIE: Doesn't matter. It'll take hours. You know what—

GUS: Sure?

LAURIE: Sure. Open it, please, would you?

WAITER: Yes, sir.

GUS: I'm sure he'd change it if we ask him.

MARGARET: Laurie would die. Of embarrassment apart from anything else.

LAURIE: It's all right, leave it. I'll do it.

WAITER: One whisky sour.

ANNIE: Thank God for that. Thank you.

GUS: That's all for the moment. Oh—Perrier? Yes. Here you

      are, Margaret.

WAITER: Thank you, sir. Good evening.

GUS: Good evening.

      (WAITER *goes out*.)

DAN: I don't think he approved of us much.

LAURIE: Did you think so? Yes. I had that feeling.

MARGARET: Thinks we're alcoholics.

LAURIE: I thought he thought the girls were probably O.K. But
      not us.

ANNIE: Perhaps he thinks we're none of us married.

GUS: Oh, yes—having a real mucky weekend, gang bang stuff.

LAURIE: He looked very suspiciously at you.

GUS: Did you think so?

LAURIE: I noticed it. Thought you were a bit effeminate I expect.

GUS: Perhaps he did. I think it's these bloody trousers, darling.
      You said I should throw them away. They don't do much
      for me do they?

LAURIE: Nothing desirable.

ANNIE: Darling, you always look rather effeminate. You and
      Laurie both do. In different ways.

GUS: Ah, but Laurie carries it off somehow. I don't.

MARGARET: Especially to foreigners.

ANNIE: It's part of your masculine charm.

GUS: What do you mean?

ANNIE: Oh, I don't know. A kind of mature softness.

MARGARET: And peacockery.

ANNIE: Yes, a bit uneasy sometimes but gallant and foursquare
      all the same.

LAURIE: Doesn't sound too bad.

ANNIE: It's lovely.

GUS: You're quite right. I know foreigners think like that. It's
      hell when I'm in America.

LAURIE: They think I'm Oscar Wilde. It's very flattering.

MARGARET: And don't you play up to it!

LAURIE: Well, I mean you just have to, don't you? It's like they
      expect to see the Changing of the Guard.

ANNIE: Thank heavens for the charm and feminity of the English
      male I say.

LAURIE: Well, American women certainly don't have it. Poor sods.

MARGARET: I'll drink to that.

LAURIE: Perrier. Ugh!

MARGARET: I like it.

LAURIE: Everyone's glass charged? Right . . . Well, here we all are.

ANNIE: Here we all are.

LAURIE: Here's to all of us. All friends and all together.

MARGARET: Well, naturally.

LAURIE: No, it's not natural. It's bloody unnatural. How often do you get six people as different as we all are still all together all friends and who all love each other. After all the things that have happened to us. Like success to some extent, making money—some of us. It's not bad.

GUS: Bloody good.

LAURIE: Everyone's married couples nowadays. Thank heaven we're not that.

MARGARET: You're drunk already.

LAURIE: You know what I mean.

MARGARET: Yes.

LAURIE: To us, and may the Good Lord bless and keep us.

ALL: To us.

LAURIE: And preserve us from that dinosaur film producer.

ANNIE: I don't think I can quite drink to that.

GUS: It's a problem.

LAURIE: Well, suit yourselves . . . Ah, that's better.

GUS: Isn't it good?

LAURIE: All right, Amy?

AMY: Fine.

ANNIE: Guilty?

AMY: No. I'm forgetting it until Monday.

ANNIE: I wonder if you will.

LAURIE: Well, give her a chance. Dan?

DAN: Smashing.

ANNIE: You know what: I think people who need people are the ghastliest people in the world.

LAURIE: Absolutely. We all just happened to find one another.

At the right time.

ANNIE: It sounds a bit Jewish show biz.

LAURIE: I thought it was a rather tense Anglo-Saxon sentiment myself. I mean you couldn't sing it.

ANNIE: Well, you could. It would be rather mediocre.

LAURIE: I mean you couldn't belt out a rather halting little comment like that. It's not poetic. It's just a smallish statement. About six unusually pleasing people. Well five. God, I'm getting fat.

MARGARET: You've always been fat.

LAURIE: Really? *Have* I? I've deceived myself.

MARGARET: You're very attractive. Pleasing.

LAURIE: More pleasing than K. L?

MARGARET: Yes. Don't know about more attractive.

LAURIE: Hell!

AMY: We really *are* lucky. I mean it's a splendid hotel and a lovely suite.

DAN: Which *you* can't afford.

LAURIE: You don't have to. *I* can. So can Gus. You made all the arrangements. And Dan's going to do all the talking.

AMY: I think they all speak English.

LAURIE: You must admit it's better than that rotten Paris.

ANNIE: I suppose we're all what's called spoiled.

LAURIE: What do you mean: spoiled?

ANNIE: Well, first class hotels, great suites, anything we want to drink.

LAURIE: What's spoiled about that? I'm certainly not spoiled. I work my drawers off and get written off twice a year as not fulfilling my early promise by some philistine squirt drumming up copy, someone who's got as much idea of the creative process as Dan's mother and mine rolled into one lazy minded lump of misery who ever battened off the honest efforts of others.

ANNIE: Writers are born to be reviled.

LAURIE: No they're not. They sit in judgement on themselves all the time without calling in outside help. They need to be loved and cared for and given money.

ANNIE: We all love you and you make lots of money.

LAURIE: Where would K.L. be without me—where *will* he be
without me to write his lousy pictures? Pretty all right, I
guess. And without Gus to edit them into making sense
and cover up his howlers? Of course, I suppose you'll go
on doing it.
(*Pause.*)
LAURIE: Well, not this one. Besides, he hates it if I make money.
I think he tips off the tax man. We don't live in Switzerland
any of us do we? More sense but still. . . . Loaded with
distinction and not a C.B.E. to go round. When I think
of the rotten dollars I've made—
MARGARET: Don't.
ANNIE: And K.L.
LAURIE: Well, lolly doesn't worry him. He spends it. You just
round up a few people like Gus and me here, turn them up on
the gas and if you suck around the blood counter at the
supermarket, long enough, you've produced another picture,
And you go on doing. What I do, I get out of the air. Even
if it's not so hot always, I put my little hand out there in
that void, there, empty air. Look at it. It's like being a
bleeding conjuror with no white tie and tails. Air . . .
MARGARET: Hot.
LAURIE: It never pays what it costs . . . No. I'm feeling quite
relaxed now. Sure you won't drink?
MARGARET: I do keep telling you.
LAURIE: Sorry. Actually, I do speak Italian quite beautifully,
don't I, darling?
MARGARET: The accent's good.
LAURIE: Poor vocabulary. But they don't mind if you make it
up. They love it. (*All very fast but clear.*) Prego, prego. Si,
grazie. Signorina. E machina bella. Grande film con
regissori K. L. con attirci Inglesi tutte bellisima. Attrici
Inglesi molto ravissante crumpetto di monde. Per che. Me
Lauri scritori Inglesi famioso connossori, grosso. Molto
experementi, Senza pommodori, si. Oggi declarimento
attrice Inglesi crumpetto elegante, insatiabile, splendido
lasagne verde antifascisti pesce Anna Magnani Visconti
arrividerci con rubato grazie mille, grazie. There, wasn't

that good! Allemange basta! Pasta per tute populo. Kosygin pappa mio. Si grappa, per favore.

MARGARET: I think I'm going to sort the rooms out.

LAURIE: Oh, leave it.

MARGARET: I want to unpack.

LAURIE: Oh, all right.

MARGARET: And I expect the others do. Unless they want an Italian lesson.

LAURIE: Shall we go to an Italian restaurant tonight?

GUS: That sounds good. Darling?

ANNIE: Perhaps we should try the local hostelries.

LAURIE: Yes. I expect you're right. I'm too fat for wop food.

MARGARET: Dutch food's rather heavy.

GUS: Enormous portions. Good beer. I've got an information thing here.

ANNIE: Oh heavens—don't start on that already.

GUS: Well, we'll have to make a decision.

LAURIE: I don't see—

GUS: Might have to book a table or something. If we want to get somewhere good.

LAURIE: Yes, I see.

ANNIE: You both make it sound so difficult.

LAURIE: My dear Annie, it *is* difficult. I can't think of anything that comes easily. It's all difficult.

ANNIE: You need one of those things that fortifies the over forties.

LAURIE: I'm not over forty!

MARGARET: Well, you look it.

LAURIE: What are you trying to do to me?

MARGARET: No, you don't. You look like a teenager.

LAURIE: Yes, a plump, middle-aged, played out grotesque.

ANNIE: Never believe in mirrors or newspapers.

LAURIE: I thought I'd got the mirror fixed . . . I need another one after that.

MARGARET: Come on, let's explore this place and see what we've got for our money. Annie?

(ANNIE *follows her. Also* GUS *who looks helpful.*)

LAURIE: Over forties. I heard a disc jockey the other day

introducing a pop version of "Roses of Picardy".
"Picardy" he said. "Where's that?" Help . . .

DAN: Do you ever look to see if your birthday's listed in The Times?

LAURIE: Always.

DAN: And is it?

LAURIE: They missed me out the year before last. Seemed like an obituary only no notice. When you do something, try to do something, take a look at someone else's efforts, you ask yourself, *I* ask myself: is there something there that wasn't there before? Well . . . I picked this damned paper up and it seemed I hadn't even been born any more. . . . Do you ever have a little lace curtain in front of your eyes? Like little spermy tadpoles paddling across your eyeballs? No? Do you think it's drink or eyesight?

DAN: Drink.

AMY: You ought to watch that.

LAURIE: I've been watching it for years. Fascinating. And tell me, do you ever either of you, no you wouldn't Amy, but you Dan, do you ever wake up with your finger tips all tingly and aching?

DAN: No.

LAURIE: Well, do you ever wake up with an awful burn in the stomach?

AMY: Yes, he often does.

LAURIE: And then what do you do?

DAN: Get up. Work. Paint if it's light.

LAURIE: This is about five o'clock is it?

DAN: Usually.

LAURIE: And you can actually work can you?

DAN: Not always.

LAURIE: Do you wake up, Amy?

AMY: I usually wake up.

LAURIE: And then?

AMY: I make coffee or give him a glass of milk.

LAURIE: And have a bit of a chatter?

DAN: That's it. Until it's time for her to get off to K. L.

LAURIE: I'm afraid I usually need a drink. It's the only thing that burns it out. Need to weld my guts with a torch. Then about nine, it eases off. I read the post. Try to put off work. Have a so-called business lunch. That's a good waste of time. Then I know I'll have to sleep in the afternoon.

AMY: Does Margaret get up when you're like that.

LAURIE: She can't—poor old thing. You see she can't get off to sleep. So by the time I'm about to totter about downstairs, reading last night's evening papers, she's only just managed to get off. Especially now.

AMY: When she's pregnant?

(LAURIE *motions her silent at the word.*)

LAURIE: So, I'm afraid we're a bit out of step with sleep. When I was eighteen I used to sleep fourteen hours on Sundays. When my mother would let me.

DAN: My mother made too much noise.

LAURIE: If *only* you can find enough energy. Where do you find it? Where's the spring?

AMY: You're loaded with it. You've got far more than Dan.

LAURIE: No, I haven't. Dan doesn't need energy. He runs perfectly efficiently on paraffin oil. You fill him up once a year and he's alight for another twelve months. With me, I need the super quality high-thing stuff poured into my tank twice a day. Look at K. L. He's unstoppable, you never have to wind him up. He just goes. Like that.

AMY: He gets very worn out.

LAURIE: I should think he does. If I did what he does in a day, I'd be in bed for a month.

DAN: He delegates.

LAURIE: Ah, yes—the operator's alchemy. Where do you get it? He takes it from *us*. We could be giving it to one another. He's been draining our tanks, filling his own. Filling up on all of us, splitting us up.

(MARGARET, ANNE *and* GUS return.)

MARGARET: Give what to each other.

LAURIE: A little vitality.

ANNIE: We're all right. And we're on hols. So we can re-charge.

LAURIE: Yes, we've got away.

ANNIE: The rooms are fine. You and Margaret are having that one. Gus and I this one and we decided Amy and Dan would like that one with the view. It's nice.

AMY: Are you sure?

ANNIE: They're all nice. Now we can get our stuff in.

MARGARET: Gus has done nearly all of it already. Gus, you are a darling. Honestly, you two! Letting Gus do all the carrying.

LAURIE: Good for his figure.

MARGARET: Typical.

LAURIE: And bad for my kidneys.

MARGARET: Are you going to help me unpack?

LAURIE: Do you want me to?

MARGARET: No, I don't think so.

LAURIE: I can.

MARGARET: I don't doubt it.

LAURIE: Shall I talk to you while you do it?

MARGARET: No. Talk to Dan and Gus. I might lie down for a bit.

LAURIE: Let me—

MARGARET: Please stay where you are.

ANNIE: Ours won't take a second.

LAURIE: You seem to have brought an awful lot of stuff. What are you going to do? Play golf? Hunt or something?

ANNIE: Mostly Gus's stuff. Medicines, all chemists counter.

DAN: Got my easel?

AMY: Yes.

DAN: Right. Just in case.

(ANNIE *and* AMY *go to rooms.*)

I'll never use it.

LAURIE: Working on your own. I could never live on my own. Oh, I have done. It's been all right for a time. But what about now and then, the steep drop and no one there. And no one to phone or too far away.

DAN: Or too early in the morning.

LAURIE: That's one of the few good things about movies. You do work with others. Bit like the army.

GUS: I suppose we really have made the right selection? Over the rooms?

LAURIE: Who cares? They'll all be the same.

GUS: I just thought Margaret ought to have a nice one. If she's not sleeping.

LAURIE: Gus, I know you mean well but please forget about it. I say, old Amy won't get the sack when she gets back to K. L?

DAN: No. He relies on her too much.

LAURIE: Do you mind?

DAN: Mind?

LAURIE: I shouldn't think you see much of her. His nibs keeps her at it. Seven days a week.

DAN: He pays her well. More than I earn. It works out.

GUS: Don't think that would suit me.

DAN: Annie can't see all that much of you.

GUS: Oh, a fair bit. He tries to keep me away from her, mind you. You know: don't bother to drive home. Stay here and we can make an early start at breakfast. But I hardly ever do. I need a bit of looking after, I'm afraid. I hate staying in other people's houses. Unprepared and all that. No shaving stuff. Or someone else's. And I don't like really sleeping on my own. Somehow, well the quality of sleep is different. Do you know what I mean?

DAN: I can sleep anywhere.

LAURIE: I think I know. More drink—before they come back?

GUS: Well. It does seem a bit unfair to drink so much in front of Margaret.

LAURIE: It isn't. But just don't say so.

GUS: Oh? All right. Well, here's to all of us. Amsterdam . . . What a brilliant idea of yours. He'd never think of here.

LAURIE: No?

GUS: Not exactly his sort of place I'd have thought. Not much night life.

DAN: Few bank managers dancing with each other and that's it.

MARGARET (*off*): Laurie. Would you ring down for some more Perrier for me?

LAURIE: O.K. darling.

(*He hesitates, looks hopefully at* GUS, *who responds.*)

GUS: I'll do it.

LAURIE (*grateful*): Oh, would you? Thanks. (*He pours out for* DAN.)

GUS (*on phone*): This is room 320. Yes. Oh, yes—room service, please . . . Hullo, can I have two large bottles of Perrier water. And, oh, yes some ice. And a bottle of Cutty Sark. You brought Haig last time. Yes. Thank you. All fixed.

LAURIE: Thanks. And no one's to buy an English newspaper. Right?

DAN: Right. It's not your birthday is it?

LAURIE: I wonder why she didn't ring down herself.

GUS: Unpacking, I suppose . . .

DAN: I was thinking the other day: do you think they make bicycle clips any more?

LAURIE: Hadn't thought of that. No, of course. All those little bare black ankles.

GUS: Bicycle clips . . . I think I've still got mine.

LAURIE: Like Picardy I should think. No one would know. Like those things you used to wear on your sleeves.

DAN: I should hope not.

LAURIE: Well, of course, I never did. I'll bet *you* did.

GUS: What?

LAURIE: Wear those things. Up here.

GUS: No— I don't think so.

LAURIE: Do you have one of those little pocket diaries? You know for appointments and things.

GUS: Yes.

DAN: No.

LAURIE: Well then, Gus. I wonder if this happens to you. You know how just after Christmas and you've got nothing to do except feel ill and miserable and dread those last days of December? If you haven't got to hell out of it. Well, I always start my new diary off before the New Year. Put my licence number in it because I can't remember it. Why *should* I remember it? Then you put in your telephone numbers—I even put my own in. Otherwise I might ring one I had years ago . . . Well, and then there are the names of all those people, not all those people but some people

106

because I don't keep many in there and then you know—
every year I sit down and there's not just one I don't put
in again, there's four, five, six. I think there are only about
eleven in this year—and that includes people like you and
Dan and K. L. *He'll* be out next year. And my agent. And
that's about it. Oh, and my mother . . . Hey, what are you
all doing in there?

ANNIE (*off*): Unpacking!

MARGARET (*off*): What do you think?

LAURIE: Well, come back in.

AMY: Coming!

LAURIE: Margaret! We're all missing you. We're on our own.

MARGARET (*off*): No, you're not. You're getting stewed.

LAURIE: We're six and there are only three in here.

ANNIE: Bad luck.

LAURIE: We love you. Why have you gone and left us? We came
here to be together. And you all disappear off to the
bedroom or the bathroom and dolly about with your rollies
and skin tonic. Come back in here! You're needed!

GUS: Yes, come back. Annie!

ANNIE (*off*): I'm unpacking all your laxatives and pouve juices.

AMY (*appearing*): All done! It's a lovely room, Dan. Go and
look at the view.

DAN: I will.

LAURIE: You deserve a lovely room, my dear. Come here and
give me a kiss. Just for arranging everything if for nothing
else ever. Not a hitch.

AMY: It was easy. K. L.'s got a good travel agent.

LAURIE: You didn't use *him*!

AMY: He won't let on. I briefed him.

LAURIE: Good girl. Well, if you lose your job, you'll have to
come and work for me. Have a drink. Won't be as exciting
as K. L. But you'll get more time off.
(*Knock on door.*)
That's *him*. He's found out where we are. You've bungled
it and he got on a plane and did it the quick way.

AMY: Come in.

LAURIE: Scusi, scusi. Momento, momento, tutte in bagno.

Basta, per favore.

(WAITER *enters*.)

WAITER: Whisky sour?

LAURIE: No, Cutty Sark.

AMY: Annie, did you order a whisky sour?

ANNIE (*off*): Yes. I knew you'd all forget me.

GUS: Why didn't you tell me? I've ordered.

ANNIE (*entering from bedroom*): Easier. Thank you.

GUS: I ordered. Cutty Sark. And Perrier. And ice. You won't forget!

WAITER: Very well, sir. (*Goes.*)

GUS: Crossed lines. All right, darling?

ANNIE: Everything's out. Anything from bowels to athlete's foot.

LAURIE: Do you know there really is such a thing as writer's cramp?

ANNIE: Sounds rather comic—like housemaid's knee.

LAURIE: Not funny if you're a housemaid or a writer.

DAN: Have you had it?

LAURIE: Naturally. What's more I get psychosomatic writer's cramp.

AMY: You can type. I've seen you.

LAURIE: The commitment's too immediate. Horrifying. Like kissing someone for the first time and then bingo you're having to slap the breath of life into some rotten little fig of a human being that heaved its way between you five seconds afterwards. Do painters get anything like housemaids?

ANNIE: Aching backs I suppose on murals and things. Do you?

DAN: Not much.

LAURIE: That's because you work at a controlled pace, you see. Everything you do has rhythm, you see. Systematic, consistent. *That's* the thing. Mine's all over the place.

ANNIE: You produce the goods.

LAURIE: Are—but do I then?

ANNIE: Don't fish. You know you do.

LAURIE: But what goods? I ask myself: can anything manufactured out of this chaos and rapacious timidity and scolding carry on really *be* the goods. Should it not be, I

108

ask myself. What do I ask myself, perhaps I shouldn't be rhetorical and clutter conversations with what-do-I-ask-myselfs? Won't the goods be shown up by the way of the manner of their manufacture? How can they become aloof, materials shaped with precision, design, logical detail, cunning, formality. And so on and so on.

ANNIE: And so on. You're not such a bad tailor.

LAURIE: No, I'm not.

ANNIE: There, you *were* fishing.

LAURIE: *And* I provide my own cloth. Any clunkhead can cut. I don't mean in your sense, Gus.

GUS: What? Oh, no—you're right.

ANNIE: I've a feeling we're getting back to K. L. *You* said let's leave him behind. But you won't.

AMY: He will.

GUS: Well, it is difficult you must admit. He rather makes one talk about him.

ANNIE: Perhaps we should go straight back to London and be with him after all.

GUS: Don't suppose he'd have us altogether.

ANNIE: Why were you doing your parliamo Italiano bit?

AMY: He thought it was K. L.

ANNIE: *That* would have fooled him!

GUS: You didn't really did you?

LAURIE: No. Except with him nothing is so awful he couldn't visit it on you.

ANNIE: No one would think you'd been loving friends for ten years.

LAURIE: You can't be loving friends with a dinosaur.

ANNIE: What are you then?

LAURIE: A mouse—what else?

ANNIE: Some mouse. With the soul of a tiger.

LAURIE: A mouse. With the soul of a toothless bear.

ANNIE: What's Gus?

LAURIE: Gus? He's, he's a walking, talking, living dolphin.

ANNIE: Amy?

LAURIE: An un-neurotic fallow-deer.

ANNIE: And Dan?

LAURIE: Dan, he's a bit difficult. Rather cool, absent-minded but observant. Orang-utan.

ANNIE: Me?

LAURIE: You're a rather sophisticated mole who keeps pushing up the earth to contract all her chums in the right place at the right time.

AMY: And Margaret—what's she?

LAURIE: Don't know. That's a difficult one.

GUS: Something frightfully attractive but efficient.

LAURIE: A rather earnest chimpanzee. Practical, full of initiative.

ANNIE: Inquisitive?

GUS: I don't think chimpanzees are very attractive.

ANNIE: Neither are moles.

LAURIE: Oh, yes they are. I'd love a mole for Christmas. Perhaps you can buy rubber ones in Amsterdam.

DAN: I don't think Orang-utans and what was it, fallow-deer, are very well matched myself. It's the sort of thing a marriage bureau computer would come up with.

ANNIE: I don't think he was very good at all.

LAURIE: Dinosaur was good.

GUS: That was easy.

ANNIE: And you didn't characterize your dinosaur.

LAURIE: I will.

ANNIE: Don't. We know.

LAURIE: Perhaps he's not the same dinosaur to all of us. It's obvious but it may be his little tiny dinosaur's trade trick.

(MARGARET *enters*.)

MARGARET: Was that the waiter?

GUS: Wrong order. Your Perrier's coming.

MARGARET: You rang down?

LAURIE: Yes. We did.

MARGARET: We?

LAURIE: Gus did. It's the waiter—he likes rough trade, don't you, Gus?

(GUS *grins*.)

It's the beatings at that prep school and scrumming down in the mud and being genuinely liked by the men, no?

GUS: I don't think the waiter's exactly my dish. But I quite like

110

the Dutch I think. Seem rather nice up to now.

ANNIE: We've not taken much of a sample. Taxi drivers, receptionists . . .

LAURIE: Air hostesses. International. But I think we're going to like the Dutch. I think we're going to have a lot of time for the Dutch as my horrible mother says.

ANNIE: Only means nasty contraceptives to me. And chocolate.

LAURIE: What, you mean chocolate coated ones? Oh, I see. Talking about that arse aching subject, somebody told me only very bovine girls can munch away at 'em. Air hostesses are made for the pill, for instance. Will you have a pill with your coffee madam, with the airline's compliments. *They* take them. If you've any temperament at all, you just kick around in your stall like a racehorse. I mean you couldn't *give* the pill to racehorses.

DAN: Well, it would be doping them, wouldn't it?

GUS: I say, this is *good*, isn't it.

ANNIE: Don't say it—we're really here.

LAURIE: Well, we are.

(*Knock at door.*)

ANNIE: Come in.

(WAITER *comes in.*)

(*to* LAURIE.) Sorry. I thought we'd had enough of your Italiansprache.

GUS: Ah! Good evening. (*As if he hadn't seen the* WAITER *before.*

WAITER: Sir. (*He put things down.*)

(*Pause.*)

GUS: Where would you recommend us all to eat on our first night in Amsterdam?

WAITER: It depends on what you have in mind.

GUS: Well, what we have in mind is absolutely the best, not necessarily the most expensive or the most famous. I mean: what would you suggest?

WAITER: It's difficult, sir. There are many excellent places to dine.

AMY: I've got a typed list here, Gus. More or less in order.

GUS: I just thought he might—

LAURIE: I should forget it.

GUS: What?

LAURIE: Amy's well trained. She always gets out a list of the six-supposed best restaurants for K. L. I've often wondered what he'd have done if his surname had been Young or Yeo or Yarrow.

GUS: Why?

LAURIE: We'd have called him K. Y.

ANNIE: *You* would.

GUS: What's K. Y.?

LAURIE: Gosh, these prep schools were tough weren't they? Or did you use Matron's vaseline? You *do* like it rough.

GUS: Oh!

(WAITER *goes out.*)

LAURIE: Oh. You know what its legitimate, well intended use is? Cleaning surgical instruments. Well, you remember that assistant K. L. had a couple of years ago . . .

ANNIE: What happened to him?

LAURIE: Stepped on the trap door in front of the desk one day I suppose. Anyway . . .

MARGARET: I don't remember him.

LAURIE: Yes, you do. English faggot he picked up in Hollywood. About thirty-five, all tight pants and white socks and greying hair.

MARGARET: Oh, and that expression . . .

LAURIE: Yes, I think you called him the frozen Madonna. I called him Sibyl. He had a crown of sibillants over his head. He sounded like a walking snake pit. I mean, you could even hear him from one end of the Crush Bar at Covent Garden to the other—*packed*. So, Sibyl told me he went into this chemist and there was this other faggot behind the counter. He says: very dignified: can I have a tube of K. Y. please? The assistant doesn't say a word, wraps up package, gives it to him. Then as he drops his change into his palm, he says. . . . "Have fun." And Sibyl said "I looked and said 'What? Cleaning my surgical instrument?' "

MARGARET: Now, listen, I think Gus is quite right, we should have a talk about what we're going to do and then make a decision.

ANNIE: That could take hours.

MARGARET: Well, it mustn't. This is our first evening. We've made all this effort to get here and go through all these elaborate conspiracies not to let K. L. know where we are. Amy may have lost her job. *And* we haven't got all that that much time.

LAURIE: I wonder where we'll all sit down and do this again.

ANNIE: If you'd said "when" I'd have belted you.

GUS: Tomorrow. Tomorrow.

MARGARET: Oh, come on. Amy, let's look at your list. I don't think we want to go anywhere too ambitious tonight.

GUS: All right, Margaret?

MARGARET: I just think we've been travelling and getting out of London and we should go somewhere fairly quiet but very nice and—oh, I don't know. What have we got here . . .

GUS: We must go to the Rijksmuseum.

MARGARET: Yes, Gus, but not tonight. Rembrandts are for the morning.

ANNE: And there's the Stedelijk.

DAN: And those Indonesian places where you get thirty great dishes.

AMY: You're greedy.

MARGARET: This sounds the sort of thing: fairly conservative but attractive seventeenth century surroundings, beautiful tables and candles. That sounds like us. Tonight anyway. Laurie, choose.

LAURIE: They all sound good. Like the waiter said. That one you said looks pretty good.

MARGARET: Annie?

ANNIE: Yes. That sounds what we'd like. Gus doesn't like too much noise. He can't talk *and* eat.

DAN: Anything will do us.

MARGARET: Right. Then let's get the concierge to book a table. As there's six of us. And it may be busy.

LAURIE: I'm on holiday. Amy will do it.

MARGARET: We're all on holiday. Why should she do it?

AMY: I'll go and ring down. Give me the list. (*Goes off to bedroom.*)

GUS: Then we'd better talk about tomorrow. What people want to do. I mean some may just want to sleep or do nothing.

MARGARET: No. I don't think that's right. We should try and all do the same thing. Unless . . . Well, we'll see what everyone says.

ANNIE: I can tell you what everyone will do—just talk. About what to do, where to go, what we should wear to do it. And we'll end up getting drunk at lunchtime in the American Bar and eating in the Hotel Dining Room.

LAURIE: Sounds delightful.

GUS: I suppose it isn't very adventurous.

MARGARET: Annie, you'll have to help me.

LAURIE: We're here—that's adventurous.

ANNIE: We'll talk about tomorrow over dinner.

GUS: I'll bring my guide.

MARGARET: Amy!

AMY: Yes?

MARGARET: I know nobody knows we're here but we might get one call for this room. If we do it'll be for me. Perhaps you should tell them. Save confusion.

LAURIE: For you! But we agreed not to tell *anyone* we were here. Except the blooming nanny and she wouldn't get through. Who did you tell, for God's sake?

MARGARET: Gillian.

LAURIE: What did you go and tell your bloody sister we were here for?

MARGARET: Oh, don't be silly. I told her not to tell anyone we're here.

LAURIE: But what did you tell her *for*? She's not one of us.

MARGARET: Isn't she?

LAURIE: Well, she's not really anything to do with K. L. And, besides, she wouldn't like it. She thinks we're all a bit flippant and middle-aged. Not half as middle-aged as her.

MARGARET: Come on. You like her. It's just that she's been having a bad time lately.

LAURIE: What bad time?

MARGARET: I'm not sure. But this affair she's having——

LAURIE: Oh, fleecing another rich duke of £500 and clenching

114

her fists because she didn't lose her cherry until she was twenty-eight and she doesn't think she gives satisfaction and she plays Bach fugues all night and doesn't wash her hair because it's all so difficult. Blimey! I think *I* complain. She needs a public recognition for the suffering she undergoes, that's all. Then she'll feel better. She should get the Golden Sanitary Towel Award. K. L. can give it to her at the Dorchester with all the past winners present.

MARGARET: Well, I told her if things got too bad to ring me.

LAURIE: You didn't say she could come here?

MARGARET: I said if things got too much, for her, I'd get her a room.

LAURIE: Oh, lovely for your friends.

MARGARET: I don't think anyone will mind.

LAURIE: Did you ask them?

MARGARET: You don't have to ask friends everything.

LAURIE: Perhaps you do. If she comes out, we can all go home. Why don't she and K. L. get together?

MARGARET: She's my sister, Laurie. I'm not having anything happen to her. Just for want of a phone call.

LAURIE: She won't do anything to herself. Not till it's too late. Like getting laid.

MARGARET: I love her.

LAURIE: You can. Don't expect your friends to.

GUS: Poor girl. What is it?

LAURIE: She's just a star wrecker of other people's coveted, innocent little weekends, that's all.

GUS: Oh, if she turns up, we'll look after her. She can't spoil anything. It's all right.

ANNIE: Of course it is. I know how to deal with Gillian. Put her to bed, that's the best thing.

LAURIE: It's a long way to come to go to bed. I mean, I know people go to New York for haircuts——

MARGARET: Let's not argue, darling. I'm sure it won't happen. She doesn't want to worry me.

LAURIE: She wants to worry everybody.

ANNIE: Listen, Laurie, darling. We're together. We've got days ahead. No one knows where we are. Except your daft nanny. Now—

GUS: She's right. Oh, I'm sure that restaurant's first class and tomorrow we'll do just as we like and go round the Leidseplein and Rembrandtsplein and the discotheques and clubs. . . .

ANNIE: Drink up, Laurie. You'll feel better.

LAURIE: I shall, I shall. I feel better already.

GUS: Old K. L. wouldn't like this at all. He'd have wanted to be out on the streets by now. Not just sitting around talking. What *would* he do?

ANNIE: Oh, exhaust a list three times as long as Amy's in half the time. Play games into the night. Games with victims.

GUS: I mean he'd hate this. Just us: talking among ourselves.

LAURIE: Well, as we're all here because of him, because of him, let's drink to him. Don't go yet, Amy. Ladies and gentlemen, to our absent friend.

MARGARET: What's the time?

AMY: Six o'clock.

GUS: He must have rung somebody by now.

MARGARET: Perhaps we should have a little zizz before we go out to dinner.

ANNIE: Good idea.

GUS: He may not know we're *all* gone yet.

LAURIE: Not together, anyway.

ANNIE: I should think he'll go off to Paris or something. Anything. And when we get back just manage to make us feel foolish. We'll just say we went away for the weekend. Do we have to tell him everything? What am I saying?

MARGARET: What about Amy?

ANNIE: That's up to her.

LAURIE: Oh, he'll be adroit. But he'll also be maladroit. He won't be able to resist trying to discover where we've been and who with.

ANNIE: Perhaps he just won't care. As you said, it's not exactly his idea of fun. God, he'd be pleased and amused.

LAURIE: Oh, he'll appear to be innocent, rational, ill-used. Slightly impatient.

116

GUS: The trouble is he creates excitement.

LAURIE: Not half enough.

GUS: Perhaps we're all second rate and need second rate excitement, sort of heats one's inadequacies.

LAURIE: He takes nothing out of the air round *his* head. Only us. Insinuates his grit into all the available oysters. And if ever any tiny pearls should appear from these tight, invaded creatures, he whips off with them, appropriates them and strings them together for his own necklace. And the pearls have to be switched or changed about. Otherwise the trick, the oyster rustling would be transparent and the last thing he wants made known is his own function or how he goes about it. Where does he get the damned energy and duplicity? Where? He's tried to split us up but here we are in Amsterdam. He has made himself the endless object of speculation. Useful to him but humiliating for us. Well, no more, my friend. We will no longer be useful to you and be put up and put down. We deserve a little better, not much but better. We have been your friends. Your stock in trade is marked down *and* your blackmailing sneering, your callousness, your malingering, your emotional gun-slinging, your shooting in the dark places of affection. You trade on the forbearance, kindliness and talent of your friends. Go on, go on playing the big market of all those meretricious ambition hankers, plodding hirelings, grafters and intriguers. I simply hope tonight that you are alone—I know you won't be. But I hope, at least, you will feel alone, alone as I feel it, as we all in our time feel it, without burdening our friends. I hope the G.P.O. telephone system is collapsed, that your chauffeur is dead and the housekeeper drunk and that there isn't one con-man, camp follower, eunuch, pimp, mercenary, or procurer of all things possible or one globe trotting bum boy at your side to pour you a drink on this dark January evening . . .

ANNIE: Well—Amen.

GUS: Gosh—it's started to snow.

LAURIE: I think I'm the only one who believed all that. Good, all the better. We can get snowed up.

117

MARGARET: Well, I'm going to have a zizz.

GUS: Yes. I should. And we can discuss the alts later.

LAURIE: Oh, yes we'll discuss them.

MARGARET: Laurie?

LAURIE: Just finish this.

MARGARET: We don't want to go out too late.

AMY: I'll book the table.

(They go to their rooms.)

ANNIE: Think I'll have one too.

LAURIE: Finish your drink first. I am glad it's snowing. How I hate holidays. Those endless, clouded days by the pool even when it's blazing sun. Do you remember doing it? All together—at K. L.'s villa? We drank everything you could think of from breakfast onwards after that vile French coffee. The deadly chink of ice in steaming glasses all day. Luxury, spoiled people. Lounging together, basting themselves with comfort, staring into pools. A swimming pool is a terrible thing to look into on a holiday. It's no past and no future. You can stare into a stream or a river or a ditch. Who wouldn't rather die in a ditch than in a pool? I'm too fat for pools and the pretty girls with their straps down and their long legs just make me long for something quite different. I always want someone to write me long, exhilarating love-letters when I lie there with the others . . . A handwritten envelope by your towel, curling up.

GUS: We didn't get on too well that time, did we? I'm sure it wasn't our fault.

ANNIE: We played too many games—too many bloody games, expected too much of the sun and each other and disappointed K. L. . . .

GUS: He asked us all again.

LAURIE: Yes. I read somewhere that one of those communications people, the men who tell you what it is we're all feeling now because of *the* media, said that marriage and romanticism was out. At least with the young people.

ANNIE: I suppose it was on the way out when we came in.

LAURIE: I wonder where we ought to go to live. All those sleepy-eyed young mice squeaking love, love. Scudding into one another, crawling over each other, eyes too weak for bright light, tongues lapping softly . . . all for love, a boy's tail here, a girl's tail there, litters of them.

DAN: Think I'll take a look at my things. (*He goes out.*)

GUS: Is he all right?

ANNIE: Yes. You know Dan.

LAURIE: I think he may be a very violent man.

GUS: Dan?

LAURIE: Fools make him suffer. So he paints or reads a book.

ANNIE: Or goes into his fallow-deer.

LAURIE: Don't blame him.

GUS: Well, perhaps you'd better come with your whatever-I-was.

ANNIE: Yes.

GUS: So, shall we say seven-forty-five? First drink. Well, not first drink, really.

LAURIE: Nineteen-forty-five hours. First drink.

GUS: Good. Where's my street guide? (*He goes.*)

LAURIE: Ought to have a bath I suppose.

ANNIE: Not sleepy?

LAURIE: Yes. I wish I could live alone. Do you?

ANNIE: No. I never have.

LAURIE: I have sometimes. It can be all right for weeks on end even. But then. You have to crawl out of the well. Just a circle of light and your own voice and your own effort. . . . People underestimate Gus I think.

ANNIE: So do I.

LAURIE: Do you think *you* do?

ANNIE: I don't think so.

LAURIE: He doesn't exhilarate you like K. L.?

ANNIE: No.

LAURIE: No. Gus has created himself. Thinks he's nobody, thinks he behaves like it. Result: himself.

ANNIE: Do you think Margaret's all right?

LAURIE: No.

ANNIE: Can I do anything?

LAURIE: She doesn't like being pregnant.

119

ANNIE: Who does? A few mooish ladies.

LAURIE: She feels invaded, distorted. About to be destroyed.

ANNIE: Why do you both do it then? Was it the same with the others?

LAURIE: I thought we might get pleasure from it. She thought I would get pleasure.

ANNIE: And you haven't?

LAURIE: Perhaps they're like holidays or hotels.

ANNIE: No. Not hotels. You couldn't live without them.

LAURIE: I love Gus very much. I think he really believes most people are better than him . . . I only suspect it.

ANNIE: He loves you.

LAURIE: Good. Try not to be too restless. Don't do that. What were we all doing this time last year? I mean were we all together or separate?

ANNIE: Separate.

LAURIE: I wonder *what* we were doing. We'll have a good evening. I feel better already. The snow's stopped.

ANNIE: Good. Seven-forty-five then. Try and kip. (*She kisses him lightly.*)

LAURIE: I will. And you, Annie. And you.

(*She goes to her room, taking her handbag. The three doors are closed.* LAURIE *looks out of the window.*)

CURTAIN.

120

ACT TWO

The same. Two evenings later. They are all in the sitting room, looking much more relaxed, enjoying the First Drink of the Evening.

GUS: Well, what's the schedule for this evening?

MARGARET: I don't care.

AMY: Neither do I. Everywhere's been good.

LAURIE: I know. Isn't it weird?

ANNIE: Why shouldn't they be?

GUS: Yes, well if we came up with an absolute dud at this stage we could hardly complain.

MARGARET: I must say that list of yours has been infallible.

LAURIE: Brilliant.

DAN: All smashing.

GUS: Not a dud. I say, we really have had quite a time, haven't we? Friday evening seems weeks away. So does K. L. Right after the first evening. Not a foot wrong. We're jolly lucky.

LAURIE: I mean even that Indonesian place was quite funny.

DAN: Actually, it was a "lovely feast of colour".

MARGARET: All those dishes. How many do you think we actually got through?

AMY: I think Dan had a bit of the whole thirty or whatever it was.

LAURIE: Still looks as lean and clean as a brass rail.

MARGARET: And we got Laurie round to the Rikjsmuseum, without too much bitterness.

LAURIE: I felt at home in all that non-conformist gothic.

ANNIE: And there *were* the Rembrandts.

LAURIE: Yes. We needed a drink after that. I keep thinking of him watching his house being sold up. All those objects, all those pieces and possessions got with sweat, all going. K. L. would have enjoyed that.

ANNIE: Don't be unfair.

121

LAURIE: And his child dead. What was his name? Titus?

ANNIE: I liked the place with the bank managers dancing together.

LAURIE: That's because you danced with that chamber-maid from Hanover.

ANNIE: It seemed only fair. It's a bit churlish to just go and gawp like a tourist. I think you were very mean not to dance.

LAURIE: No one I fancied.

MARGARET: Annie's right. You got frightfully stuffy and absent minded all of a sudden.

LAURIE: I was worried about you and that lady in the black dinner jacket.

MARGARET: You didn't show it. I don't know what I'd have done if Gus hadn't protected me.

ANNIE: She really fancied you, didn't she?

AMY: I'll say. I've never seen anything like it.

DAN: She was just queer for pregnant girls.

MARGARET: I'd have thought that would have put her off.

GUS: Not at all.

ANNIE: What about tonight?

GUS: Yes. We must make a decision.

ANNIE: Where's the list, Amy?

DAN: Let's have a look. What are the alts?

GUS: We've still got lunch tomorrow.

LAURIE: Why don't we stay the extra day?

ANNIE: We've done all that.

MARGARET: Yes. Amy must get back.

LAURIE: But why? I don't see it.

MARGARET: Because she doesn't want to lose her well paid job, which she also likes.

ANNIE: And she has obligations.

LAURIE: What obligations? You don't have obligations to monsters.

DAN: What about this? I don't know . . .

AMY: Why don't we go to the place we went to on the first evening?

LAURIE: That was wonderful.

122

DAN: At least we know it's first rate.

GUS: You don't think that being a bit unadventurous do you?

ANNIE: Yes. Let's chance our arm.

LAURIE: Why should we?

MARGARET: I agree. We should try something different.

DAN: What for? Not that I mind.

LAURIE: You girls are so ambitious. Even if it's for others.

GUS: Really escaped, didn't we? I haven't laughed so much for
    months. Have you, darling? You said last night.

LAURIE: I still think we should go back a day later.

MARGARET: No.

LAURIE: Amy could fix it.

AMY: Of course. Why don't you? I could go. It seems silly
    when you're having such fun. Dan, you could stay with
    them.

ANNIE: I think we've voted on that one.

LAURIE: Oh no we haven't. I wonder when we'll all sit down
    like this again.

MARGARET: Damn it, we've done it enough times before.

ANNIE: Sure, we'll do it again.

LAURIE: Yes. But when? How? Where? How do we arrange it? I
    don't want to go back to London.

ANNIE: Who does.

LAURIE: No. I mean it. What is there there for any of us? We
    should all go and live together somewhere.

MARGARET: Where, for instance? Somewhere you didn't have to
    pick up the phone for room service.

LAURIE: We need a broken down Victorian castle or something,
    oh with all the plumbing and jazz we wanted. But lots of
    space around us. Acres of land around us, empty, chipped
    and scarred still by Roman legions.

ANNIE: Sounds freezing.

LAURIE: What would you prefer, a sonic bang up your lush,
    southern parkland? We could do what we liked, have lots
    of children.

GUS: There aren't many of us.

LAURIE: We'll think of some others.

ANNIE: But who?

GUS: K. L. would find out about it.

LAURIE: Let him. You'd all come, wouldn't you?

ANNIE: What about staff?

MARGARET: Good question.

DAN: You'd need lots of nannies.

LAURIE: Yes. Well . . . we'd get ex-stewardesses from El Fag Airlines. They're absolutely wonderful nannies. Poor old things will work for absolutely nothing if you get a really rejected one.

AMY: And the rest of the staff?

LAURIE: They must be people we know. People who'd fit in with everyone. I would learn carpentry. I've always wanted to do that. And brick laying. I could work on the house. Gus knows all about electricity. Margaret could drive. Except we wouldn't use the car much. Annie's the great horse expert. We could use them and maybe hunt if we got over our green belt liberal principles. And Dan could, well he could just paint.

GUS: Who do we know?

LAURIE: Well, we ought to make a list. That's one thing, do you realise, we've escaped from? Margaret? My relatives and all those layabout people I pay to look after us. So that, the thoery being, we are able to do other things, not bother with inessentials because we've *made* it.

ANNIE: I thought your Nannie was good?

MARGARET: She's very good.

LAURIE: Only she doesn't look after *me*. She looks after two creatures who don't even know yet they're being waited on.

ANNIE: I thought you didn't like being waited on.

LAURIE: I don't. But if I pay for it at home I expect it.

AMY: They're only tiny babies.

LAURIE: Darling, don't say "tiny babies". All babies are tiny compared to people. Even if they had to be landed like killer sharks, they're still tiny. What I hate about them, it's like my relations and K. L., you always, you're expected to adjust to *their* mood, their convenience, their bad back, or I-don't-know-I'm-just-depressed. What are they going to be like when I ring the bell, when I open their letters.

They never anticipate *you*.

ANNIE: Gus never anticipates for himself.

MARGARET: How?

ANNIE: He's always taken by surprise by situations and people's reactions.

MARGARET: Laurie rehearses them all.

GUS: Am I?

ANNIE: He was cutting some trees down just by the pond one day. And he'd keep stepping back. Just about a foot away from the pond. "You will mind the pond" I'd say to him. "What? Oh. Yes." Then he'd do it again. "Don't forget the pond." "No . . . all right" . . . Always a bit surprised. I watched him for two days and then I thought I can't go on. I'll leave him to it. He missed it by inches for a whole morning. And then fell in.

GUS: Yes. That's quite right. I did feel surprised when it happened.

LAURIE: The mistake is to feel guilty. That's always been my mistake. He's driving you about because you're cleverer than he is. And though I say it, he can't even drive as well as I can. That's why he's a servant, she says. Well, why can't he be a good one, I say. I wouldn't want him to wait on me. I don't know though. Why do it at all? There are third rate servants. Perhaps I've got the ones I deserve, like the relatives I deserve.

DAN: As the old saying goes, we're all bloody servants.

LAURIE: You're right. Deliver the goods or the chopper. I suppose that's right. Do we deliver the goods?

ANNIE: If someone's cooked you a meal decently and woken you and been able to smile as well, that would be delivering the goods.

MARGARET: It would.

LAURIE: *Are* we spoiled?

ANNIE: Staying in a luxury hotel on the continent because you're afraid of your servants?

LAURIE: That does make it sound stupid. Very.

GUS: But that wasn't the main reason.

LAURIE: Yes. I just send my nasty relations a cheque. I never see

125

them. They certainly don't want to see me.

DAN: What are they?

LAURIE: Retired rotten, grafting publicans, shop assistants, ex-waitresses. They live on and on. Having hernias and arthritic hips and strokes. But they go on: writing poisonous letters to one another. Complaining and wheedling and paying off the same old scores with the same illiterate signs. "Dear Laurie, thank you very kindly for the cheque. It was most welcome and I was able to get us one or two things we'd had to go without for quite some time, what with me having been off work all this time and the doctor sends me to the hospital twice a week. They tell me it's improving but I can't say I feel much improvement. How are you, old son? Old son? We saw your name in the paper about something you were doing the other day and the people next door said they thought you were on the telly one night but we didn't see it, and Rose won't buy the television papers so we always switch on to the same programme. Rose doesn't get any better, I'm afraid. I brought her a quarter bottle the other day with your kind remittance which served to buck her up a bit. Your Auntie Grace wrote and said she'd heard Margaret was having another baby. That must be very nice for you both. We send our best wishes to you both and the other little ones. Hope you're all well. Must close now as I have to take down the front room curtains and wash them as Rose can't do it any longer, but you know what she is. Bung ho and all the very best. Excuse writing but my hand is still bad. Ever. Your Uncle Ted. P.S. Rose says Auntie Grace said something about a letter from your mother which she sent on but I'm afraid she sent it back unopened. She just refuses to pass any comment. She told me not to say anything about it to you but I thought I'd just—*PASS IT ON TO YOU!*"

(*He gestures towards them.*)

Pass *that* on!

MARGARET: Oh, don't talk about them. They're so depressing.

ANNIE: They sound quite funny.

126

LAURIE: They're not quite funny, Annie. They're greedy, calculating, stupid and totally without questions.

MARGARET: They're just boring.

LAURIE: They're not that even. They're not even boring. Now *I* am boring. I am quite certainly the most boring man you have ever met in your lives. I see you're not going to contradict me so I won't let you.

GUS: As a matter of fact, I was going to contradict you because I am infinitely more boring than you could ever be even on a bad day. Not that I think you could be even then.

MARGARET: You're both drunk.

LAURIE: No, we're not. At least Gus may be a bit. I am just straightforwardly boring. Look, some people when they're drunk are dreadfully boring, especially when they're supposed to be freewheeling and amusing. Now, drink doesn't do that to me. Drink doesn't change one, does it?

ANNIE: Not much.

LAURIE: There you are. I am just as boring drunk as I am sober. There is no appreciable difference. If I could tell you, if I could, how much I bore myself. I am really fed up with the whole subject . . . I am a meagre, pilfering bore.

DAN: Well, don't be a bore and enlarge on it any more.

LAURIE: You're drunk! (*Laughs.*) I say Dan's drunk. We really are having a time. . . .

MARGARET: Did you see Terry had married that girl friend of K.L.'s?

ANNIE: Yes.

DAN: Not that horrible Tina Whatsaname?

AMY: The same.

LAURIE: That's the movie business. Where the producer persuades the director to marry *his* crumpet.

MARGARET: He hasn't got a very strong character.

LAURIE: What does that mean?

ANNIE: I think he'll survive her.

LAURIE: I mean K.L.'s got a *strong* character. Hasn't he? Does it mean simply someone who can impose their will on others? Can be politic and full of stragegy!

MARGARET: You know what I mean about Terry.

LAURIE: I saw something very interesting the other day. No, somebody told me.

AMY: About air hostesses?

LAURIE: No, about nurses. Is this boring? That's the window sign of a bore. He always says to you at some point, is this boring?

ANNIE: Fascinating.

LAURIE: Yes, well I think it probably is. Because it may affect us all in some way. Well, apparently if you've got the real incurables, the carcinoma or some dance like that going on inside you, the doctors very sensibly start pumping things into you at the right time and make you as thumpingly stupid as possible. Unfortunately, the nursing profession being imperfect, like El Fag Airlines or any other concern contains a considerable and dangerous fifth column of popish ladies in starched collars and cuffs who'll fail to give you your shot of blissful dope come six o'clock. Nothing to call on in the small house but a couple of codeine and an Irish lilt. So, do you know what they do, the clever ones, the doctors? Well, if they should decide they'd rather a patient didn't lie in agony, they insist on a roster of Australian nurses. They're the best. The Aussies. They'll give you enough for you and your horse if you tell 'em. So, if you ever wake up after you've been in hospital for a little while and one day a little cobber voice says to you "And how are we today, Mr. so-and-so?" you know you've scored.

ANNIE: Yes. That's better than the lady pilot.

LAURIE: Annie?

ANNIE: What?

LAURIE: You're called Annie and I'm called Laurie.

ANNIE: What are we suppose to do?

MARGARET: Hadn't you thought of it before?

LAURIE: No. Isn't that odd? Had you?

GUS: Not me. I don't think. Annie mentioned it to me one day.

LAURIE: Dan?

DAN: I've got used to it. The trouble with being spontaneous, or even trying to be, and I think one can, the trouble is it

128

does put you at the mercy of others. That's not the same thing as being a bore.

LAURIE: What do we ever go back to England for? What do we do it for?

ANNIE: I thought you never wanted to come away.

LAURIE: It's the bitchiest place on earth.

MARGARET: That's the name of the place you come from. Now, what have we decided?

GUS: About what?

LAURIE: We haven't decided anything. Um? (*Holds her hand.*)

MARGARET: I mean where are we going for our last night?
(*Knock on door.*)

LAURIE: You didn't order anything, did you?

GUS: No.

AMY: Probably the maid with all those clean sheets for when we go.

ANNIE: Come in.
(*The door handle rattles.*)

GUS: No key. Well, if it's K.L., he's too late. We've done it.
(*He goes to the door, opens it. A girl of about thirty,*
GILLIAN.)

LAURIE: Gillian.

MARGARET: Darling.

GILLIAN: I'm sorry. I should have warned you.

MARGARET (*to her*): My darling, what's the matter? You look ill.

GILLIAN: I didn't have a chance. I'm all right. I couldn't remember how long you were staying.

MARGARET: Why didn't you ring me? Come in and sit down. Take your coat off.

GILLIAN: No. I think I'll keep it on.

LAURIE: Oh, sit down and take the bloody thing off. It's hot in here.

GILLIAN: I'm sorry. I should have rung first. I couldn't find the number.

LAURIE: Just the name of the hotel?

MARGARET: Laurie, give her a drink.

GILLIAN: No, I'll have a Perrier.

LAURIE: Don't tell me *you're* pregnant.

MARGARET: Give her one.

GILLIAN: Just a small one, very small.

LAURIE: Did you bring your own nose dropper?

GILLIAN: Well, how are you? Have you had a good time?

LAURIE: Fanfuckingtastick! Never stopped laughing, have we?

AMY: We've had a marvellous time. Why didn't you come?

GUS: I think you'd have enjoyed it. We've done quite a lot in an easy sort of way, done what we wanted——

LAURIE: After dicussion.

GUS: After discussion. And all the places we've been to have been tremendous fun—thanks to Amy's list.

DAN: I liked that place like the Brasserie at Joe Lyons where everyone sang Tipperary—in English.

GUS: Yes, I think you'd have liked it—don't you, darling?

ANNIE: I don't think she'd have liked that place much, Margaret didn't.

GUS: Oh well, Margaret didn't feel so hot for a while.

MARGARET: I just can't stand the smell of beer and all those awful swilling, ugly looking people.

ANNIE: I think the men enjoyed it rather more.

AMY: I loved it.

DAN: You even sang—as usual.

LAURIE: What do you mean—the men liked it?

ANNIE: I mean you sometimes try and fumble your way back to childhood while we watch and get impatient and wait for you to stop.

LAURIE: Perhaps you should try coming along.

ANNIE: Yes. We found two really remarkable restaurants, we discovered a new game, or rather Laurie invented one, and Gus had us in stitches telling us stories about his regiment in the war, with two versions to every story, one tragic and one comic, the tragic one always being comic and the comic one always tragic. Laurie's starting a new airline and Dan's putting out a new scent. They'll tell you.

GILLIAN: I'd like to go to the Rijksmuseum.

LAURIE: There are other things here besides Rembrandt. We needed a drink after him. Drink?

GILLIAN: Thanks.

130

LAURIE: Too much?

GILLIAN: No fine.

LAURIE: Only I don't want you leaving any because I'm an
impoverished writer with a wife, children, useless servants,
a family of ageless begging letter writers, a trencherman
nanny and three dogs as big as you. I haven't yet found
my voice, I write too much not enough, I have no real
popular appeal, I take an easy route to solutions——

ANNIE: Stop being paranoid.

LAURIE: Why? If a man is ill he isn't a hypochondriac. And if
he's attacked he's——

MARGARET: Oh, shut up, Laurie. Can't you see there's something
the matter?

LAURIE: Who with? Annie?

GILLIAN: I told you—honestly—everything's fine. I just thought
I'd come suddenly.

MARGARET: Darling, I've known you all my life. Something's
very wrong. Do you want to tell me?

LAURIE: Oh, leave her be.

MARGARET: I know her. You don't.

GILLIAN: I wish I *had* come. You all look as if you've had a
super time.

LAURIE: I'll bet we do—now. (*To* MARGARET.) You're right—it's
not a very convincing performance.

GILLIAN: Tell me what else you've been doing. It does sound
good. I've always wanted to come to Amsterdam.
(*She leans forward avidly. The others decline visibly. She has
broken the fragile spell.*)
Did you go on the canal?

DAN: Yes.

GILLIAN: And that modern art gallery, whatever it's called. Can't
pronounce Dutch. And the harboar, or where is it, where
all the tarts sit in the windows looking like dolls. This hotel
looks splendid. They were terribly nice downstairs. They
seemed to know all about you lot up here. They smiled the
moment said who I wanted. Do you think I can get a
room? Perhaps I could get one down the hall. All I need
is a little room. I suppose I could come in here with you

131

most of the time. Don't let me interrupt what you're doing. I'll just finish this and change, I think, Perhaps I could have a bath in your room Margaret, if Laurie doesn't mind. What time are you going out? I don't want to hold you up. I needn't unpack. Unless you're dressing up. I could change in your room though and see about the room later. Do you know where you're going tonight? . . .

GUS: We were—just discussing the alts. Perhaps we should go somewhere you'd like.

GILLIAN: Don't change anything because of me. It's my fault for turning up like this. Just do what you would have done by yourselves. Please don't let me change anything . . .

LAURIE: Gillian, for Christ's sake burst into tears . . .

(*Slowly she crumples and they watch her.*)

GILLIAN: Please . . . take no notice. I'll get a room down the hall.

(MARGARET *puts her arm around her and leads her into her bedroom and closes the door.*)

LAURIE: Drink anyone?

ANNIE: Yes, please.

GUS: Poor girl.

DAN: Just as well we're going tomorrow.

AMY: I wonder what it is.

LAURIE: Oh, either her lover's married and can't or won't get a divorce or he *isn't* married and she can't bring herself to offer herself up to something total. Variations on some crap like that. But I tell you, she's not going to blight our weekend. We've had ourselves something we want to have and we made it work and she's not going to walk in here on the last night and turn it all into a Golden Sanitary Towel Award Presentation.

ANNIE: I'm afraid she's done it.

LAURIE: Well, we mustn't let her. Look, Gus, flip through that list and we'll decide where to go and either she can come with us and put on a happy face or—

ANNIE: Oh, not that.

LAURIE: No, I agree—the miserable one's better. You and Dan can talk to her a bit about the Rembrandts and painting

and Dutch domestic architecture and what Marshal
McLuhan said to Lévi-Strauss while they were on the job.
Otherwise, she can just shut up and leave us to it. Or
Margaret can stay with her arms around her in the bedroom
all evening.

GUS: That's not very fair on poor old Margaret.

LAURIE: Her sister's not being very fair to us.

ANNIE: That's not her fault.

AMY: No. Dan will talk to her and cheer her up. He's good at
that.

LAURIE: Why should he?

DAN: Sure. I don't mind.

ANNIE: Why should we? We do. Listen, Margaret will listen to
her and calm her down. Then we'll take her out with us.
She'll be all right.

LAURIE: But will we be? If I didn't know I'd think it was a
last-minute joke of K.L.'s on us. Blimey, she's turned it
into Agony Junction all right. Look at Gus. Dan, have
some more in there.

GUS: Oh, she's not such a bad girl.

DAN: She's brought London with her . . .

GUS: Perhaps we should go to the place we went to on the first
night, anyway.

LAURIE: I suppose so.

GUS: I think she'd like it. It's quiet and the food—did you have
those herrings?

AMY: My chicken in that pastry thing was wild.

LAURIE: Oh, she'll be sick or pushing her food away or leaving
it and pretending she's enjoying it and filling us up with
guilt and damned responsibility. Damn her, we've just got
together again, she's an odd man out, we haven't got time
to take off for her coltish, barren, stiff-upper quivering lips
and, and klart-on. Am I unsympathetic?

ANNIE: Yes.

LAURIE: I'm sorry . . . all of you . . .

DAN: Not your fault.

GUS: Not anybody's fault.

133

LAURIE: Beaudelaire said: can't remember now.

GUS: Someone said the other day: "What do you do if you live in San Francisco, you're twenty-one and you go bald . . ."

LAURIE: He said, I know, "beauty was something he only wanted to see once."

ANNIE: She's quite attractive.

LAURIE: Gillian?

ANNIE: Um.

GUS: Very.

AMY: Not as much as Margaret.

ANNIE: She's prettier than she thinks, that's the trouble.

LAURIE: She should take some pretty pills. So should I. I'm all water. Heavy. Bit of underwater fire like North Sea gas. Not much earth or air either . . . What a *precious* remark— that's her fault. Did I tell you about the boy with the crocodile shoes?

ANNIE: No, but it's too long. I've heard it.

DAN: Tell them the one about the nun in the enclosed order.

GUS: Wish I could remember jokes.

LAURIE: Young nun enters an enclosed order with a strict vow of silence. The silence can only be broken once every three years with two words. So: after three years the girl goes to the Mother Superior, who says: "Now my child, three years have passed since you entered the order. You have kept your vow of silence. It is now your privilege to say any two words you wish to me." So the young nun pauses painfully, opens her mouth and says: "Uncomfortable beds." So the Mother Superior says, "Right, my child, and now you may go back to your work." Three more years pass and she comes before the Mother Superior again. "You have observed the rule of this order for three more years. It is your privilege to say two words to me—if you wish." So the nun hesitates and then says: "Bad food." "Very well, go back to your work, my child." Another three years pass and the nun is brought in front of the Mother Superior again. "Well, my child, three more years have passed. Is there anything you wish to say to me?" The nun raises her eyes and, after an effort, she whispers:

134

"I want to go home." "Well" says the Mother Superior, "I'm *glad* to hear it. You've done nothing but bitch ever since you got here . . ."

ANNIE: Why don't you go in and see how Margaret's managing?

LAURIE: I don't think I'm what's wanted in there. Margaret will call if she wants me.

ANNIE: Are you sure?

GUS: Shall I knock?

LAURIE: No, leave them. Did you like her, Amy?

AMY: Gillian? I don't really know her. I felt sorry for her . . . when she was sitting there trying not to spoil everything.

LAURIE: But doing it pretty well all the same.

DAN: Why did you ask Amy?

LAURIE: Because Amy likes nearly everyone.

ANNIE: You make her sound imperceptive, which she's not.

LAURIE: No. I think she is blessed with loving kindness . . .

DAN: So—we've decided on the first night place? . . . Laurie?

LAURIE: What?

ANNIE: Yes.

GUS: Well, we thought so, Dan. Unless you'd like to suggest something else. We thought . . .

ANNIE: Discussion.

DAN: Perhaps we'd better start getting ready slowly. Amy?

AMY: Yes. Right. Now.

LAURIE: You two really are a lecherous couple.

AMY: Me?

LAURIE: Me? Yes, you two. You toddle off to the bedroom every evening twenty minutes before the rest of us.

ANNIE: Good for them.

LAURIE: Perhaps you simply organize these things better. Is that it, Dan? I'd never thought of it before. Perhaps, working efficient secretaries make the ideal wives. I mean it does need fitting in with everything else. How long have you been married?

AMY: Nine years.

GUS: Marvellous. Is it really?

ANNIE: Nine isn't so long. Some people have golden weddings.

LAURIE: Golden Sanitary Towel Weddings. I think Dan's pretty

135

formidable. I bet if you looked at his sexual graph of desire his would be steady, unchanging up there like Nelson on his column and there'd be mine bumping about among the lions.

DAN: Wish it were true.

LAURIE: Well, get along then.

AMY: Actually, I wanted to write a couple of postcards.

GUS: *Are* you? I don't think you should write postcards from here somehow. I haven't. Deliberately. It seemed like giving evidence that we'd ever been here all of us.

LAURIE: Yes. Well, go and do it, whatever it is. Only don't keep us waiting.

ANNIE: Oh, who kept who waiting last night?

LAURIE: I did.

AMY: See you then.

GUS: Seventeen-forty-five.

(*They go, closing the door behind them. Pause.*)
What'll you do when you get back?

LAURIE: Don't know.

GUS: No, *we* weren't sure. Were we, darling?

LAURIE: I've tried not to think about it.

GUS: Perhaps we should all have dinner the first night back. Where could we go?

LAURIE: I'll ask Margaret.

GUS: That new place you took us to the other week was nice. I wonder if K.L.'s discovered it.

LAURIE: Hope not.

ANNIE: I expect he has.

GUS: I wonder if he'll ring when we get in.

LAURIE: Sure to.

GUS: Perhaps he'll wait for one of us to ring him.

LAURIE: He can.

GUS: Well, it worked . . . Are you going to work as soon as you get back?

LAURIE: If I can. You?

GUS: I've got to. I should be there tomorrow really. Do you know what you're doing next weekend?

LAURIE: Margaret would know.

GUS: Perhaps we could do something.

LAURIE: Maybe. We'll talk about it on the train . . .

GUS: I think I'll go and have a bath. A *real* bath. I mean. What's the time? Yes, seventeen-forty-five. I'd better book the table hadn't I? Best not disturb Dan.

ANNIE: I'll have one after you.

GUS: What?

ANNIE: A bath, my darling.

GUS: O.K. Well, I'll have one first, then I'll run one for you and I can shave while you're in it.

ANNIE: Right.

GUS: You might as well stay and have another drink with old Laurie.

LAURIE: I'm all right. Perhaps she'd like a kip.

ANNIE: Bit late now.

GUS: Do you know what you're going to be wearing this evening?

LAURIE: No. Oh, the same as the first night I expect.

GUS: Yes. I see. I remember. Only it helps me when I make up my mind what to put on. It's that chocolaty mohair kind of thing?

LAURIE: That's the one.

GUS: That's good. Well, fine. See you then.

ANNIE: And, darling—wear your purple tie.

GUS: Are you sure?

ANNIE: It suits you.

GUS: Not too——?

LAURIE: Yes. Divine.

GUS: Oh, all right. Annie gave me that. It's awfully pretty. She's got the most amazing flair and taste in things like men's clothes. In everything, come to that.

LAURIE: Except men.

GUS: Yes. Well, blind spot in us all. I'll call you when I've run the bath, darling. And I'll put some of that oil in, shall I? If there's anything—with Gillian—you know, I can do, give a knock.

LAURIE: Go and have your bath. I want to see you properly turned out for our last night.

GUS: Right.

(*He goes into his room and closes the door. Pause.*)

ANNIE: Are you sure I shouldn't go in to Margaret? Girl stuff.

LAURIE: If you want to

(*She doesn't move.*)

You haven't been married before, have you?

ANNIE: No.

LAURIE: I have.

ANNIE: It's quite a well known fact.

LAURIE: Yes. It's like having had a previous conviction . . .

ANNIE: Of course, I lived with people before Gus.

LAURIE: Many?

ANNIE: I don't think so; some would. But I don't think it was inordinate—no. I lived with each one an inordinate time.

LAURIE: I wonder what my other wife thinks of me.

ANNIE: Has she married again?

LAURIE: Twice. I wonder what my name even means to her.

ANNIE: Ever see her?

LAURIE: No. I dread bumping into her somewhere. Even here the other night, I thought I saw her in that smart place.

ANNIE: Why do you dread it?

LAURIE: I don't think she likes me.

ANNIE: Why not?

LAURIE: I imagine I wasn't very kind to her.

ANNIE: Weren't you?

LAURIE: I don't know. I wish I could really remember. I try to. I hope not. But I'm sure I was.

ANNIE: It doesn't mean that *you're* unkind.

LAURIE: Doesn't it?

ANNIE: Oh, come, Just capable of it. Like everyone.

LAURIE: Amy is never unkind.

ANNIE: You don't want to be like Amy.

LAURIE: Don't I?

ANNIE: No . . . It will be all right . . . when we get back.

LAURIE: Yes.

ANNIE: Don't grieve.

LAURIE: Annie. Laurie. I do.

ANNIE: I know.

138

LAURIE: You live with someone for five, six years. And you begin to feel you don't know them. Perhaps you didn't make the right kind of effort. You have to make choices, adjustments, you have requirements to answer. Then you see someone you love through other eyes. First, one pair of eyes. Then another and more. I was afraid to marry but afraid not to. You see, I'm not really promiscuous. I'm a moulting old bourgeois. I'm not very good at legerdemain affairs. . . . Do you like Margaret?

ANNIE: Yes . . . Have you been unfaithful to her?

LAURIE: Yes.

ANNIE: Enjoyable?

LAURIE: Not very.

ANNIE: Often?

LAURIE: No. Not inordinately.

ANNIE: When was the last time?

LAURIE: Six months. Just a few times.

ANNIE: Before that?

LAURIE: Not for ages.

ANNIE: What's ages?

LAURIE: When she was in the nursing home . . .

ANNIE: In the nursing home? You mean, not——

LAURIE: Yes.

ANNIE: I see.

LAURIE: Are you shocked?

ANNIE: No. Surprised . . . Not really.

LAURIE: I thought you might say: men!

ANNIE: You're not men! I'd better go and change.

LAURIE: Gus'll call you. Have some more . . . I've wanted to tell you.

ANNIE: Have you?

LAURIE: No one knows. You won't tell Gus, will you?

ANNIE: I won't tell anyone. . . . Why did you want to tell me?

LAURIE: Why? Because . . . to me . . . you have always been the most dashing . . . romantic . . . friendly . . . playful . . . loving . . . impetuous . . . larky . . . fearful . . . detached . . . constant . . . woman I have ever met . . . and I love you . . . I don't know how else one says it . . . one

shouldn't . . . and I've always thought you felt . . . perhaps
. . . the same about me.

ANNIE: I do.

LAURIE: When we are all away—you are never out of my heart.

ANNIE: Nor you out of mine.

LAURIE: So there it is. It's snowing again . . . I wonder what
it'll be like in London.

ANNIE: God knows.

LAURIE: If we were going by plane, I'd say perhaps it'll crash.
Or we won't be able to take off.

ANNIE: We'll have longer on the train together.

LAURIE: Together? Yes, and we can all get drunk on the boat.

ANNIE: Perhaps we should change and go on the plane after all.
I don't know that I can face the journey with you there . . .
sorry. A touch of the Gillians.

LAURIE: A touch of the Annies.

ANNIE: I love you . . . I can never tell you . . .

LAURIE: Thank you for saying it . . . Bless you, Amsterdam.
Wouldn't K.L. be furious?

ANNIE: Because it's happened or because he doesn't know?

LAURIE: Both.

ANNIE: I think he'd be envious because it's happened. I fancy
he's suspected for a long time.

LAURIE: Do you?

(*She nods.*)

Yes. He doesn't miss much. Do you think Margaret knows?

ANNIE: I think she might. I would.

LAURIE: And Gus?

ANNIE: No.

LAURIE: Good . . . I think we need another . . .

(*He pours for them both. Looks down at her.*)

ANNIE: Don't look at me.

LAURIE: I'm sorry. I shall never be able to come back to this
place again.

ANNIE: Which?

LAURIE: Both. The hotel. Amsterdam.

(MARGARET *comes in.*)

ANNIE: How is she?

MARGARET: Oh, she's a little better. Some of it came out and, oh dear, I don't know why some people's lives have to be difficult. I'll tell you about it later. Anyway, she's resting on our bed. I thought she might be able to have a little zizz and then, if she's all right, she can come out with us. If not, I'll stay in with her.

ANNIE: But you can't do that. We must all go out, together, on our last night. You've got to.

MARGARET: Oh, we'll see. We'd better get her a room. Laurie, can you ring down and ask reception if there's a single room down the hall near us she can have?

LAURIE: O.K. Like some Perrier?

MARGARET: No, thank you, Laurie, are you all right?

LAURIE: Fine.

MARGARET: No, you're not I can see. He doesn't look well. Does he, Annie?

ANNIE: I think he's just getting a bit sea-sick already.

MARGARET: It's not that. Even Laurie waits till the same day.

LAURIE: Who is it this time?

MARGARET: What? Oh, Gillian. It's too complicated, now.

LAURIE: Nothing's too complicated now.

MARGARET: Darling, I think you started drinking too early. You started right after breakfast. . . . Oh, yes, she saw K.L.

LAURIE: Saw him. How?

MARGARET: He asked her round for a drink.

LAURIE: When was this?

MARGARET: Friday.

LAURIE: I never thought he'd ring *her*. She didn't tell him where we'd gone?

MARGARET: Yes, Laurie, I'm afraid she did.

LAURIE: She did! The stupid, dopey mare!

MARGARET: Oh, stop it, Laurie. It doesn't really matter as it's turned out. He didn't ring or *anything* did he?

LAURIE: You mean she told him the hotel, the lot?

MARGARET: You know how clever he is at winkling these things out of people. She said he seemed so concerned about us all, and she was, oh, distraught about her own weekend. He managed to convince her that we'd really

141

want him to know.

LAURIE: Don't tell me she's having an affair with him. They deserve each other. Except he'd spit her out in one bite.

MARGARET: Listen, Laurie, I'm worried about that girl. She's my sister and I love her, and I think she came very close to doing something to herself this weekend.

LAURIE: Don't you believe it. She just models for it. People like her don't go home and do it. They choose a weekend when there's someone likely to come in the flat or they don't take quite enough.

MARGARET: Don't be such a bitch.

LAURIE: Well, I am.

MARGARET: You certainly make the same noises sometimes.

LAURIE: You're sure she didn't spend the weekend with our friend K.L.?

MARGARET: She was all on her own. I should have found out she was feeling like this. I'd have made her come with us.

LAURIE: Nice for us.

MARGARET: Leave her alone. There are some problems you've never had to face.

LAURIE: I should hope so.

(*The telephone in the sitting room rings. They stare at it.* Who the devil's that?

MARGARET: Well, you'd better answer it.

LAURIE: She hasn't told anyone else where we are?

MARGARET: No. No one. She hasn't spoken to anyone. Well, pick it up.

(ANNIE *does so.*

ANNIE: Room number . . . what's this one? Three two O. Yes . . . No . . . Just a moment. It's for Amy.

LAURIE: Amy!

ANNIE: Amy! Phone! It's for you.

(*They wait.* AMY *appears putting on her dressing gown.*)

AMY: For me? How do they know?

LAURIE: I'll tell you.

(AMY *picks up the phone.* GILLIAN *appears in the doorway of* MARGARET's *bedroom.*)

AMY (*on phone*): Hullo . . . Yes . . . Speaking . . . Oh, hullo,

Paul. Yes . . . I see . . . no, wait a moment . . . let me think
. . . their number's in a bright green leather book on his
desk . . . yes, in the study . . . no, I'll try and get a plane
earlier . . . no, don't do that. . . . Stay there and I'll call
you back. (*She puts the phone down.*) That was Paul. K.L.'s
chauffeur . . . He's killed himself. He found him half an
hour ago.

(*Pause.* DAN *comes in, in dressing gown.*)

LAURIE: How did he find the number?

AMY: It was written on a pad by his desk. By his body.

(LAURIE *starts to pour drinks for them all.*

I suppose I'd better make some ticket arrangements.

LAURIE: Have a drink first. Here, sit down. Margaret.

(GUS *appears at his door.*)

GUS: Annie? Hullo. I didn't hear someone on the phone, did I?

ANNIE: K.L. has killed himself.

GUS: But how?

AMY: Sleeping pills. Sleeping pills and aspirin.

LAURIE: Come in. Have a drink. You too, Gillian. Dan . . .
Sleeping pills, aspirin, bottle of whisky, half a loaf of bread
to keep it all down . . . give the housekeeper the weekend
off, turn the extension off in your study and lock the front
door . . . Well, cheers . . .

(*Silence.*)

AMY: I think I'll talk to them downstairs from my room. Save
you having to listen. I expect you'd all like to go back
together if I can fix it?

MARGARET: Of course.

DAN: I'll come with you.

(*He follows her to their bedroom door. He says, a little drily.*)
I wonder: if we'll ever come here again?

MARGARET: What—to this hotel?

DAN: To Amsterdam . . .

LAURIE: I shouldn't think so. But I expect we might go
somewhere else. . . .

(DAN *closes his bedroom door.*)

CURTAIN.

143